NATIONAL GEOGRAPHIC

# OUR WORLD

**Series Editors**

JoAnn (Jodi) Crandall

Joan Kang Shin

**Author**

Kate Cory-Wright

NATIONAL GEOGRAPHIC LEARNING | CENGAGE Learning

Australia • Brazil • Japan • Korea • Mexico • Singapore • Spain • United Kingdom • United States

NATIONAL GEOGRAPHIC

# OUR WORLD

## Let's sing! TR: B44

*This is our world.*
*Everybody's got a song to sing.*
*Each boy and girl.*
*This is our world!*

*I say "our," you say "world."*
*Our!*
*World!*
*Our!*
*World!*

*I say "boy," you say "girl."*
*Boy!*
*Girl!*
*Boy!*
*Girl!*

*I say everybody move...*
*I say everybody stop...*
*everybody stop!*

*This is our world.*
*Everybody's got a song to sing.*
*Each boy and girl.*
*This is our world!*

Unit 1

# Exciting Sports

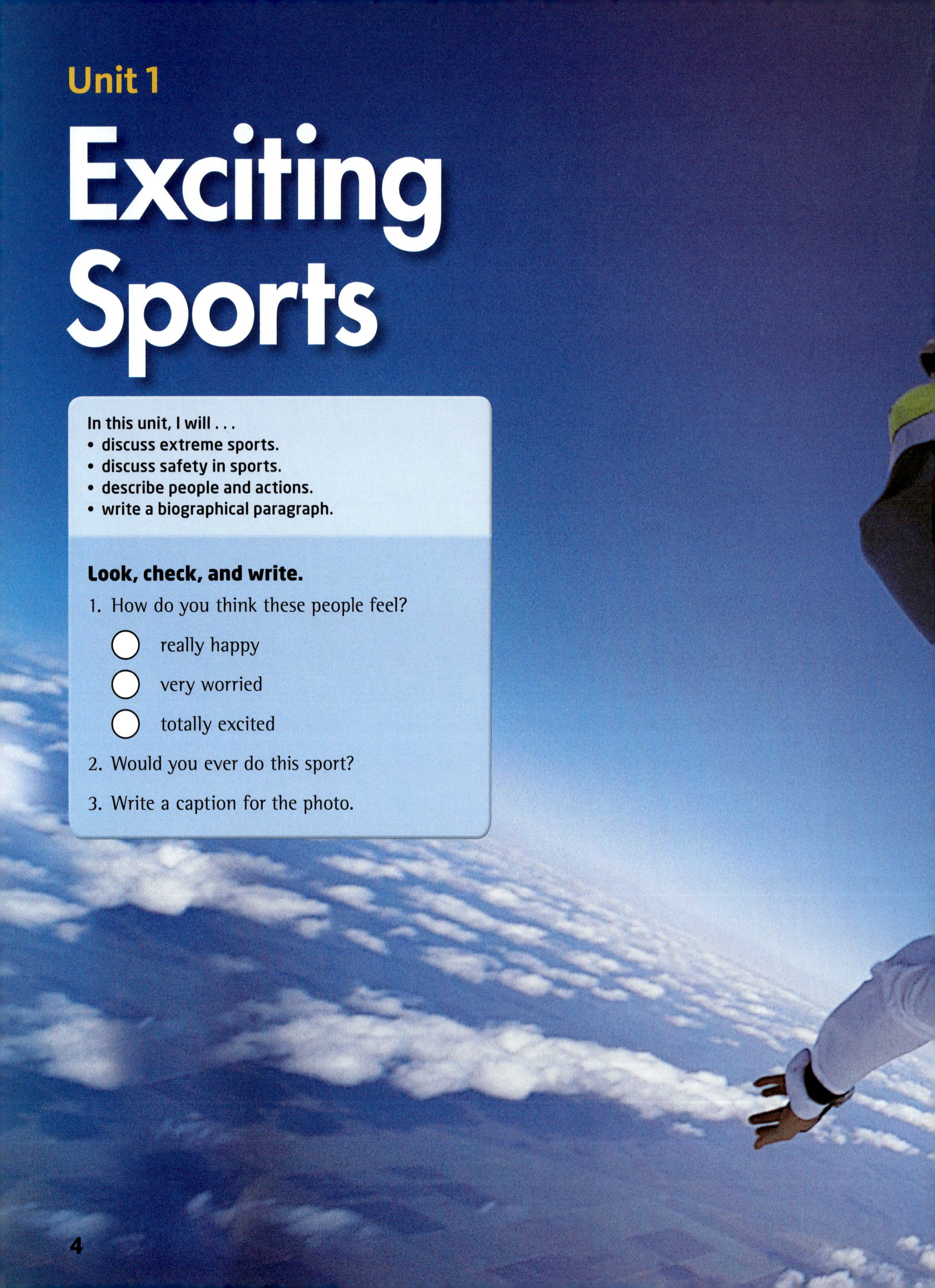

**In this unit, I will . . .**
- **discuss extreme sports.**
- **discuss safety in sports.**
- **describe people and actions.**
- **write a biographical paragraph.**

**Look, check, and write.**

1. How do you think these people feel?
   - ◯ really happy
   - ◯ very worried
   - ◯ totally excited
2. Would you ever do this sport?
3. Write a caption for the photo.

# 1 Listen and read. TR: A2

# 2 Listen and repeat. TR: A3

These days many young people do dangerous and exciting sports called "extreme sports." They can be done in the air, in the water, or on land.

Extreme skiers reach speeds of 240 km (150 miles) an hour and fly the **length** of two football fields before they **land!** Another popular land sport is BMX (bicycle **motocross**). In skiing and BMX, people **flip** in the air, like this skier!

**Kitesurfing** is a new kind of surfing. An athlete travels skillfully across the water at speeds of 55 km (35 miles) an hour or more. If he isn't **skillful**, he'll **crash**. Kitesurfers, called "Charlie Browners," need lots of **strength** in their arms.

**Hang-gliding** is one of the most popular extreme sports, although the **equipment** is expensive. Serious **accidents** are not common, but sometimes people have **injuries** when they land. Imagine flying like a bird at a **height** of 6,000 m (20,000 feet)!

skiing

kitesurfing

hang-gliding

**3** **Work with a partner.**
What did you learn? Ask and answer.

## 4 Listen, read, and sing. TR: A4

# Extreme Sports

*A kitesurfer rides the waves.*
*A kitesurfer rides the wind.*
*I've kitesurfed in my dreams*
*ever since I was a kid!*

***Extreme sports.***
***Flying high in the air!***
***Other sports***
***don't compare!***

*Extreme sports.*
*Look around.*
*They're everywhere!*

*Super cool sports!*

*Skiers flip so skillfully,*
*incredibly high above the snow.*
*I've skied in my dreams*
*ever since I was a kid.*

***CHORUS***

*Extreme sports.*
*Look around.*
*They're everywhere!*

*Super cool sports!*

*Motocross and hang-gliding,*
*are so incredibly fun!*
*I've dreamed of doing both*
*ever since I was a kid!*

***CHORUS***

*Extreme sports.*
*Look around.*
*They're everywhere!*
*Super cool sports!*

## 5 Answer the questions.

1. Circle two extreme sports athletes in the song.
2. Draw a box around two extreme sports.
3. Write an extreme sport you would like to try.

______________________________

7 **Make sentences.** Use one word in each column.

| | | |
|---|---|---|
| know | in this town | for |
| have | a computer | since |
| live | the piano | |
| study | skateboarding | |
| play | English | |
| | best friend | |
| | a bicycle | |
| | soccer | |
| | on this street | |

8 **Work in a group.** Discuss. Compare your sentences from Activity 7. Are they the same or different?

**9** **Listen and repeat.** Then read and write. **TR: A6**

1. Most skateboarding injuries happen when people do tricks and fall on the hard ground. Protect your elbows by wearing __________________.
2. If you practice water sports, you might fall in the water. Wear a bright __________________ on your body, even if you can swim.
3. When you go cycling or skateboarding, always protect your knees by wearing __________________.
4. Check your bicycle __________________ often! If they work well, you can stop your bicycle quickly.
5. BMX riders often have accidents. They should wear a __________________ so that if they fall, they won't hurt their head.

**10** **Listen and stick.** Work with a partner. **TR: A7**

| 1 | 2 | 3 | 4 | 5 |
|---|---|---|---|---|
| | | | | |

## GRAMMAR TR: A8

| | | |
|---|---|---|
| Skateboarding is | so | cool. |
| That trick is | very | exciting. |
| Those knee pads look | really | scary. |
| This boy's helmet looks | incredibly | dangerous. |
| | extremely | difficult. |
| | super | silly. |
| | totally | |

**11** **Read and answer.** Look at the picture. Then complete the sentences.

1. I think that riding a bicycle ______________________________.
2. In my opinion, skateboarding ______________________________.
3. The cyclist's trick ______________________________.
4. The skateboarder's helmet ______________________________.
5. The boy's bike ______________________________.

**12** **Play a game.** Work in a small group. Choose three sports. Write five sentences about each sport without giving the name of the sport. Exchange your sentences with another group. Guess the sports.

**13** **Listen and read.** TR: A9

# Cool Adventurers

Danny MacAskill

Danny MacAskill and Bethany Hamilton are two incredibly brave athletes who love being outdoors. Both have known success and failure in their lives.

Danny MacAskill is a skillful cyclist who flips off buildings and rides trains on his bicycle. He has often fallen out of trees and crashed since he began extreme cycling. He's been very lucky—serious accidents often happen to athletes, but he has only broken a few bones and twelve helmets. Every time he's in the hospital, he thinks of new places to ride. Born in 1985 in Scotland, he loved cycling as a kid, but he never expected to be famous. Then, in 2009, a video of him appeared on YouTube and was watched twenty-seven million times. In 2012, he became a National Geographic "Adventurer of the Year."

Super cool surfer Bethany Hamilton was born in Hawaii in 1990. She was already an extremely skillful surfer at the age of eight. But in 2003, when she was just thirteen years old, a shark attacked her, and she lost her left arm. Just one month after her injury, she was back in the water. Since then, she has learned to surf with one arm. She needs more strength in her legs than other surfers because she has only one arm, but she has won competitions. She has written a book about her accident. The book became a movie in 2011.

**Risk**

| low | | high |
|---|---|---|
| skateboarding | BMX | kitesurfing |
| cycling | surfing | extreme cycling |
| skiing | horseback riding | heli-skiing |
| hang-gliding | | |

Bethany Hamilton

## 14 **Read and write.** Read the text again.
Write **T** for *True* and **F** for *False*.

1. Danny and Bethany both do water sports. ____
2. They both continued to do their sport after they had an injury. ____
3. Bethany was in the water just one year after the shark attacked her. ____
4. Danny and Bethany are both National Geographic Adventurer of the Year. ____
5. They have both known how to do their sport since they were kids. ____

## 15 **Complete the chart.** Write the information.
Compare your answers with a partner.

| | Danny MacAskill | Bethany Hamilton |
|---|---|---|
| When they were born | | |
| Where they were born | | |
| Sport they participate in | | |
| Why they are famous | | |

## 16 **Work with a partner.**
Compare the two athletes in the text. Decide which person is braver, which is cooler, and which is luckier. Explain why you think this. Does your partner agree? Why or why not?

**weird but true** More people are killed by soda machines than by sharks each year.

## Biographical Paragraphs

A biographical paragraph describes the life of another person. When you write a biographical paragraph, you can make it more interesting for the reader if you connect the dates and events in that person's life. Words you can use to link the dates and events include: *After (that), before, since then, the next year, then, at the time, suddenly,* and *afterward.*

**17** **Read.** Read the biography. Underline the expressions that are used to link the events.

### High Climber

Before the age of nine, Matt Moniz enjoyed summer vacations like all kids do. Then his life suddenly changed. Matt's father invited him to join a climb to Mount Everest. At the time Matt did not know what to expect, but he said afterward that he had "the best time of his life." After that, there was no stopping him! The next year, he climbed two of the world's highest mountains: Africa's Kilimanjaro and Russia's Elbrus. Then, at the age of ten, he climbed Argentina's Aconcagua (a height of 6,962 meters.) Since then, Matt has climbed more mountains with his dad. In 2010, Matt became the youngest person in the world to climb the highest point in all fifty states in the U.S.—in record time. He loves the outdoors and often talks to other kids about spending more time outdoors.

**18** **Write.** Write a short biographical paragraph about someone who has an exciting job, does an exciting sport, or has traveled to exciting places. Remember to link the events and dates with connecting expressions.

**19** **Work in a small group.** Share your writing.

NATIONAL GEOGRAPHIC

# Mission

## Connect with our world.

- Work in a small group. Name some extreme sports. Group them as land, water, or air activities.
- How do you connect with nature? Write some outdoor activities that you do.

- Share your ideas with another group. Are they the same or different? Decide which ideas everyone thinks are best.

*"If you're a young person and you like to walk, climb trees, or explore, keep doing that. Because this world needs more people that are connected to Earth."*

**J. Michael Fay**
**Conservationist**
Explorer-in-Residence

Puerto Vallarta, Mexico

## 20 Plan an extreme sports camp.

1. Work in groups. Use the graphic organizer to help you describe your camp.

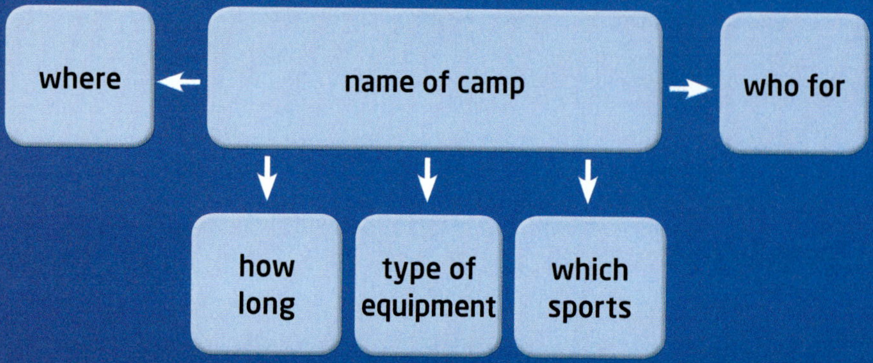


2. Make a brochure or a web page about the camp.
   a. Write a short summary about the camp. Why is it a great place for visitors or for people to spend their vacation?
   b. Add photos, pictures, and a map.

## Now I can . . .

- ◯ discuss extreme sports.
- ◯ discuss safety in sports.
- ◯ describe people and actions.
- ◯ write a biographical paragraph.

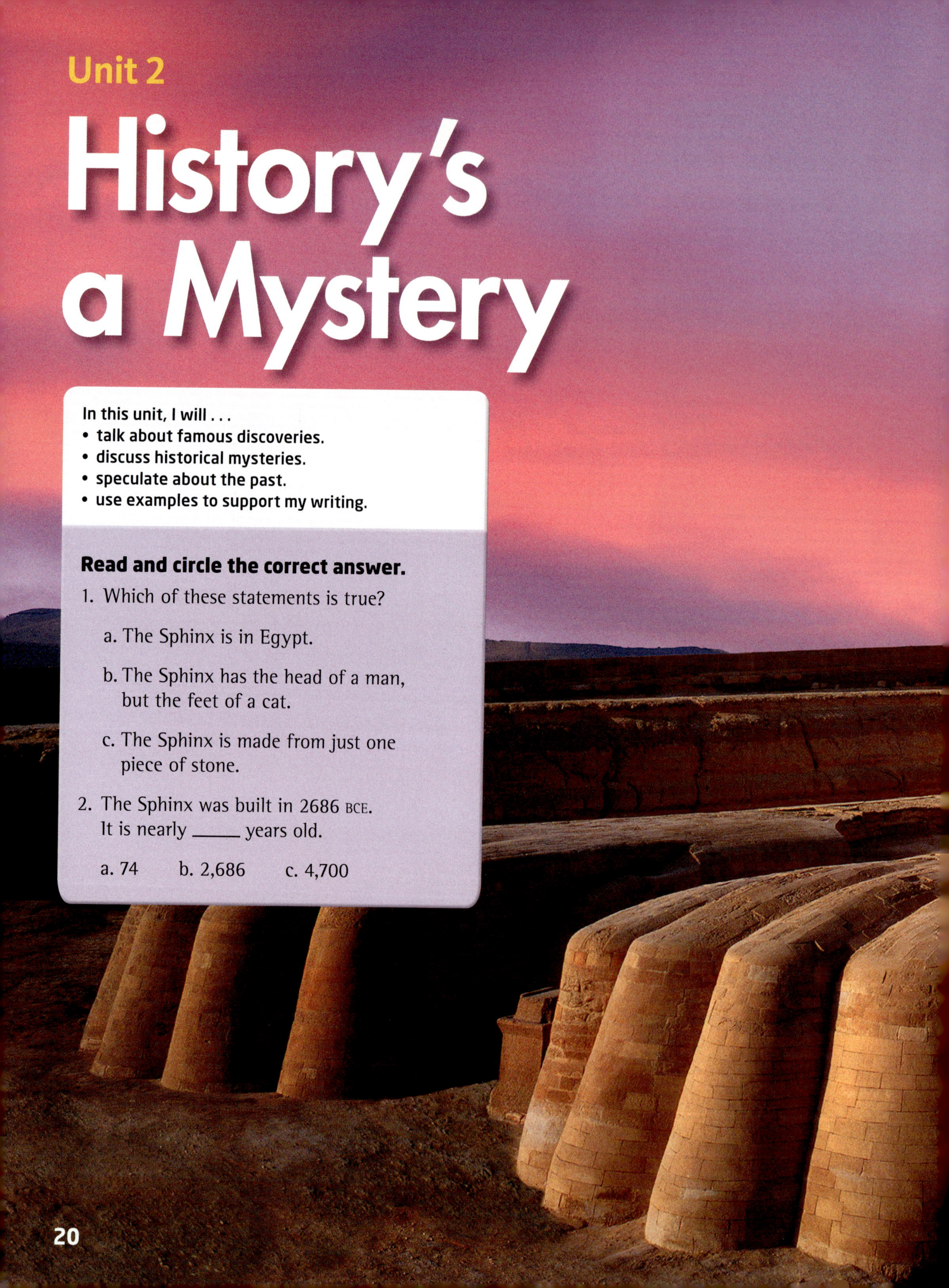

Unit 2

# History's a Mystery

In this unit, I will . . .

- talk about famous discoveries.
- discuss historical mysteries.
- speculate about the past.
- use examples to support my writing.

**Read and circle the correct answer.**

1. Which of these statements is true?

   a. The Sphinx is in Egypt.

   b. The Sphinx has the head of a man, but the feet of a cat.

   c. The Sphinx is made from just one piece of stone.

2. The Sphinx was built in 2686 BCE. It is nearly _____ years old.

   a. 74 b. 2,686 c. 4,700

The Sphinx, Giza, Egypt

1 **Listen and read.** TR: A10

2 **Listen and repeat.** TR: A11

Archaeologists have made some incredibly important discoveries—in the desert, in the mountains, and under the ground. Discoveries tell us a lot about the past.

**210 BCE**

Over 700,000 men built an enormous **tomb** for Chinese **ruler** Qin Shi Huang Di, including this army of terra-cotta **statues.** When the ruler **died,** the statues were **buried** with him in a tomb. Archaeologists **excavated** the tomb and found over 6,000 statues of soldiers and horses. Each statue is different!

a statue

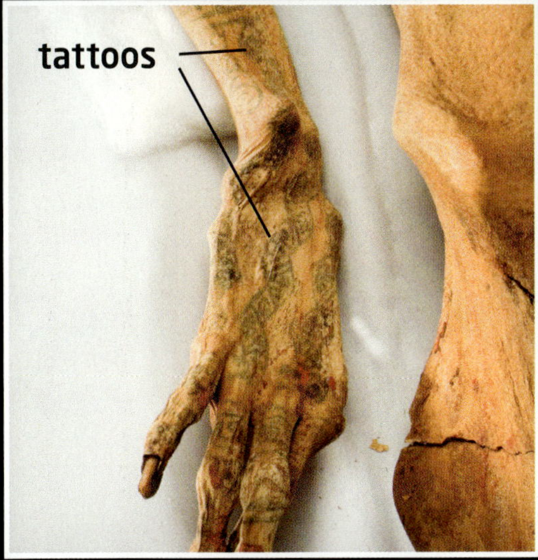

**450** CE

This female **mummy** was found in a tomb in Peru. She was beautifully **preserved,** with **tattoos** of snakes and spiders on her body. No one knows the **cause** of her death or why men were buried with her.

**650** CE

In 2009 this **treasure** was found in a field in England. Later, archaeologists **discovered** over 3,500 **objects** there. Scientists have **analyzed** what they found. They know when the **gold** was buried, but they don't know who buried it or why. Did **thieves** hide it?

**3** **Work with a partner.** What did you learn? Ask and answer.

## 4 Listen, read, and sing. TR: A12

# So Much to Learn

***History's a mystery,***
***and that's why I like history!***
***Buried statues and mummies, too!***
***So much to learn.***
***So much to do!***

*Excavated kings*
*were found by archaeologists.*
*Anglo Saxon treasure*
*was discovered*
*in the mist.*

*The Terracotta Army*
*was found deep underground.*
*Just think what you might find*
*if you look around.*

***CHORUS***

*Objects that were hidden*
*can be found by scientists.*
*Pottery and paper,*
*gold and money,*
*in the mist.*

*If we learn from history,*
*wisdom from the past*
*can help us answer questions*
*we really want to ask.*

***CHORUS***

*History's a mystery,*
*and that's why I like history!*
*Buried statues and mummies, too!*
*So much to learn.*
*So much to do!*

## 5 Check T for *True* or F for *False*.

1a. The singer thinks history is cool. (T) (F)

1b. You will be rich if you study history. (T) (F)

2. Do you like history? Why or why not?

Valley of the Golden Mummies, near Bawiti, Egypt

## GRAMMAR TR: A13

The Sphinx **was built** around 2500 BCE.
When **were** the statues **discovered?**
The treasure **was discovered** in a field.

It **wasn't excavated** until 1925.
The statues **were found** in 1974.
The treasures **weren't stolen.**

**6** **Read.** Complete the sentences. Use the words in parentheses.

1. Terry Herbert ______________________ (not/give) the gold objects. They are in a museum.
2. Some archaeologists think the Sphinx ______________________ (build) around 2500 BCE or earlier. It is made from one stone.
3. Four men ______________________ (bury) with the mummy in Peru.
4. English treasures ______________________ (not find) in a tomb. They were found in a field.
5. The terra-cotta statues ______________________ (discover) under the ground in the tomb of a Chinese ruler.

terra-cotta statues

7 **What do you know?** Write questions about a famous discovery or a place you know. Work with a partner. Answer each other's questions.

1. ______________________________

2. ______________________________

3. ______________________________

4. ______________________________

5. ______________________________

6. ______________________________

8 **Work with a partner.** Prepare a role play. Then practice and perform it for the class.

**Student A:**
You are a tourist.
Ask about a discovery or a place.

**Student B:**
You are a tour guide.
Answer the tourist's questions.

## 9 **Listen and repeat.** Then read and write. TR: A14

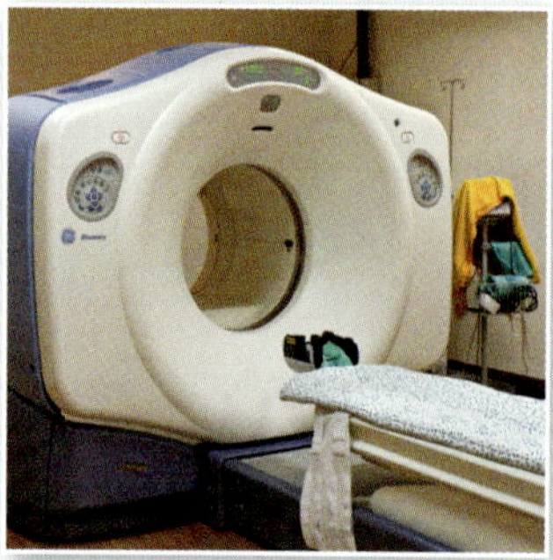

a CT scan

an artifact

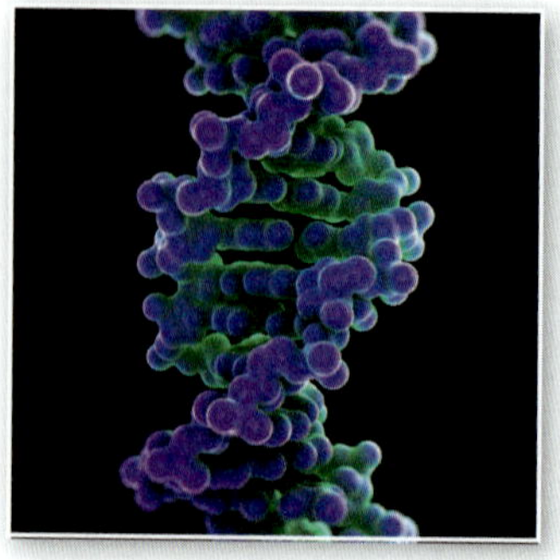

a DNA test

a site

1. Archaeologists can see inside a person's body with a ____________. This test shows if the person had any illnesses, and how they died.
2. To learn about a person's family, archaeologists do a ____________. This test tells them who the person's father was, for example.
3. We can find out what people ate before they died. We can take a ____________ of food from inside the person's stomach.
4. Archaeologists always study the ____________ where something was discovered. This helps them to learn why people lived there.
5. Archeologists often look for pottery, and other ____________ near the site. These objects help them learn how people lived.

a sample

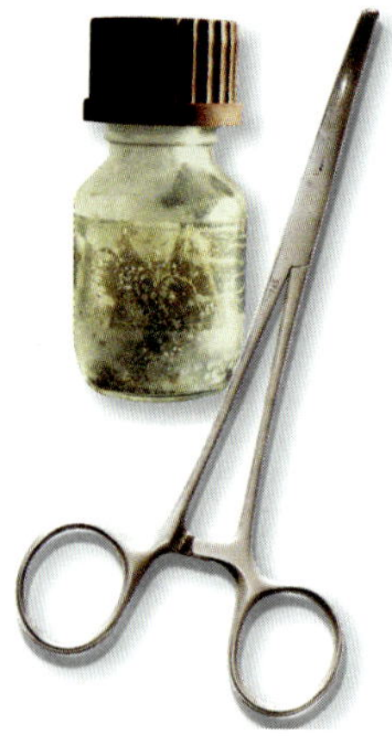

## 10 **Listen and stick.** Order the blue stickers to tell what the archaeologist discovered. Then work with a partner. Order the green stickers to say how she solved the mysteries. TR: A15

How did she discover they were from the same family?

I think she did a CT scan!

Are you sure? I don't think so.

| 1 | 2 | 3 | 4 | 5 |
|---|---|---|---|---|

## GRAMMAR TR: A16

The mummy **was found by hikers.**
The bottles **were found by divers.**
**Was** the pottery broken **by thieves?**
The tomb **wasn't found by an archaeologist.**
The bodies **weren't analyzed by scientists.**
Who **was** the treasure **hidden by?**

**11** **Read and answer.** Complete the sentences. Then listen to check your answers. TR: A17

In 1991 a mummy was discovered by (discover) hikers in the mountains. The mummy was over 5,000 years old, but he ______________ (preserve) ice. No one knows his name, so he ______________ (describe) people around the world as the "Iceman." For the next ten years, the Iceman's body ______________ (analyze) scientists. At first people didn't know how the Iceman died, but in 2001 the Iceman ______________ (study) Paul Gostner, who found an injury in the Iceman's arm. In 2005 the Iceman ______________ (check) doctors using a new CT scan machine. We now know that he died from the injury. But who ______________ (the Iceman/kill)?

**12** **Play a game.** Play with a partner. Make correct sentences to mark your X or O.

| | | |
|---|---|---|
| the Sphinx<br>analyze<br>archaeologists<br>for 37 years | the Iceman<br>find<br>hikers<br>1991 | gold objects<br>discover<br>Terry Herbert<br>England |
| the terra-cotta statues<br>make<br>70,000 men<br>China | the Sphinx<br>not<br>excavate<br>until 1925 | a mummy<br>find<br>tomb<br>Peru |
| English treasure<br>hide<br>a field<br>650 BCE | the Sphinx<br>build<br>Egyptians<br>around 2686 BCE | the Iceman's injury<br>analyze<br>doctors<br>2005 |

**13** **Listen and read.** TR: A18

# The Amazing Discovery of King Tut

Egypt is full of really exciting and ancient discoveries, but the most famous is the tomb of King Tutankhamun (King Tut). Howard Carter and another English archaeologist spent years looking for the tomb. Carter found it in 1922, after someone discovered an artifact with the king's name on it near the site. Inside the tomb, Carter found hundreds of gold objects, over 3,000 treasures, and—most importantly—King Tut's mummy. Although King Tut was buried more than 3,000 years ago, his DNA was perfectly preserved. Later, Dr. Zahi Hawass, a famous Egyptian archaeologist, moved the artifacts and the mummy to a museum.

Who was King Tut? He was an Egyptian boy who became a ruler in 1333 BCE—at the age of nine. We know from the date of some artifacts that he ruled until he died in 1323 BCE. Tut was buried with all the objects he would need in his next life. Why did he die so young? The cause of his death is not known. In 1968 his mummy was analyzed by scientists, who found broken bones in Tut's skull. A CT scan of Tut's mummy in 2006 showed that he broke his leg before he died. A DNA test showed that he had malaria. No one knows how he died. History's a mystery!

## 14 **Read and write.** Answer the questions.

1. How did Carter know where to find King Tut's tomb?

_______________________________________________

2. Why was King Tut buried with so many objects?

_______________________________________________

3. How many years was King Tut the ruler?

_______________________________________________

4. What are two possible causes of King Tut's death?

_______________________________________________

**weird but true**

**Mummy brown was a paint color made from ground-up mummies. It was used during the 16th and 17th centuries.**

## 15 **Look at the timeline.** Write complete sentences about each date.

**1333 BCE** Tut became ruler.

**1323 BCE** Tut died.

**1922 CE** Tomb was discovered.

**1968 CE** Mummy was analyzed.

**2006 CE** Broken leg was discovered.

## 16 **Work with a partner.** Choose a paragraph to talk about. Your partner will listen and take notes. Then listen to your partner talk about the other paragraph. Take notes.

| | |
|---|---|
| Howard Carter | |
| The Discovery of King Tut's Tomb | |
| King Tut | |
| Analyzing King Tut's Mummy | |

## Paragraphs of Exemplification

In a paragraph of exemplification, you give examples that support important ideas in your text. Be clear and show the reader that you know what you are writing about. To do this, add examples of facts. Use expressions like: *for instance, such as, namely, specifically,* and *a good example is.* These words let the reader know that more information is coming in the text.

**17** **Read.** Underline all the expressions that refer to examples.

### Memories from the Past

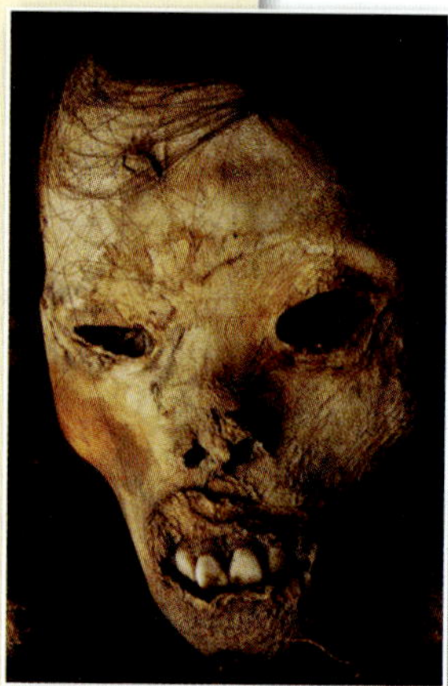

Archaeologists feel very excited when new discoveries are made because each new discovery tells them more about the past. A good example is the famous Iceman mummy discovered in 1991 by hikers in the Alps. Thanks to DNA tests, CT scans, and artifacts found near the site, we know more about people who lived long ago, namely, what they wore and how they lived. The Iceman tells us a lot. So does the famous Peruvian female mummy. For instance, we know that women were given tattoos. We also know from the mummy's tomb that men were buried together with important women (before she was excavated, we thought that only women were buried with important men). Although we still don't know everything about these mummies (specifically, the cause of their death), the Iceman and the Peruvian mummy are two incredible discoveries that tell us more about the past.

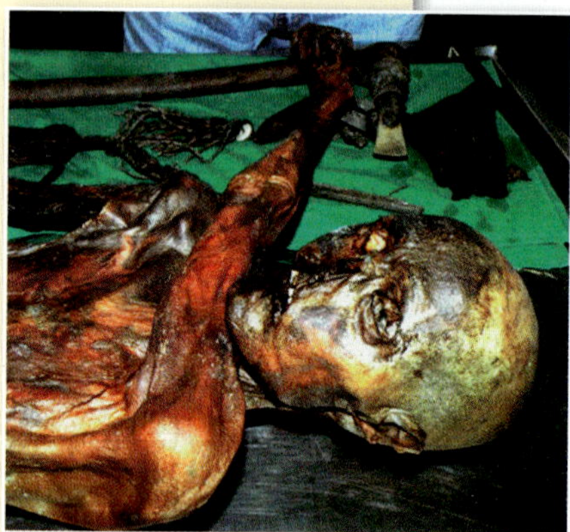

**18** **Write.** Write about the terra-cotta statues and King Tut's tomb. What do these two discoveries tell us about the past? Use examples from both.

**19** **Work in a small group.** Share your writing.

NATIONAL GEOGRAPHIC

# Mission

## Learn about local history.

- Work in a group. Is it important to protect historical places in your country? Why or why not? Discuss.
- Which places are of historical interest in your area? Who can you talk to in order to find out more information? Discuss and write the best ideas in the box.

- Work with another group. Share your ideas. Are they the same or different? Which idea does everyone like best?

*"I decided that I wanted to learn more about civilizations of the past and about people living totally different lives from mine. I could not believe my luck when I found there was an actual profession for this type of work—anthropology."*

**Johan Reinhard**
**Anthropologist**
Explorer-in-Residence

Johan Reinhard on summit of Nevado Ampato, Peru

## 1 Listen and read. TR: A19

## 2 Listen and repeat. TR: A20

One thousand years ago, chocolate was so valuable that it was used as money! Now we use chocolate every day and on special **occasions,** such as International Chocolate Day on September 13.

Chocolate comes from the cacao tree that grows near the equator. After four years, the trees start to produce **pods.** Farmers open the pods and take out the seeds. **Vanilla,** sugar, **cinnamon,** and other **spices** are added to the ground up seeds.

The **origin** of chocolate is interesting. As early as 2,000 years ago, people of the Americas were mixing cacao beans, water, and spices to make a drink. In 1502, Christopher Columbus brought cacao beans back to Spain. People later learned how to change chocolate from **liquid** to **solid.** And by 1847 they were enjoying chocolate **candy bars!**

Today there are thousands of **types** of chocolate candy bars. We have milk and dark chocolate in fun shapes, some with delicious **fillings** like **caramel.** We have **hot chocolate,** chocolate ice cream, cereal, cookies, **milk shakes,** cocoa **powder,** and even chocolate sculptures!

**3** **Work with a partner.** What did you learn? Ask and answer.

## 4 Listen, read, and sing. TR: A21

# Hot Chocolate

*Hey! Do you like hot chocolate?*

***Put some chocolate in a cup.***
***Get some milk and heat it up.***
***Stir in some vanilla. Add some spice.***
***Sprinkle on some cinnamon.***

*It'll taste right!*

*I was making hot chocolate*
*in the kitchen one night.*
*My grandma was telling me*
*I wasn't doing it right.*

*She was telling me about her mother.*
*About how she made cocoa when she was young.*
*She was telling me to sit down,*
*when she said, "I'm going to show you how it's done."*

***CHORUS***

*Hot chocolate in a cup.*
*Hot chocolate! Pour it to the top.*
*Hot chocolate tastes so good.*
*I learned to make it like Grandma said I should.*

*I love hot chocolate!*

***CHORUS***

*Hot chocolate in a cup.*
*Hot chocolate! Pour it to the top.*
*Hot chocolate tastes so good.*
*I learned to make it like Grandma said I should!*

*Hot chocolate!*

## 5 Answer the questions.

1. Who taught her to make hot chocolate?

_______________________________

2. Circle five ingredients she puts in it.
3. Do you know how to make hot chocolate?

## GRAMMAR TR: A22

By 250 CE people **were drinking** hot chocolate.
We **were** still **talking** about chocolate **when** the bell rang.
**Was** the cocao tree **growing** in Africa by then?
No, it wasn't. But it **was growing** in Africa by the late 1800s.

**6** **Read.** What were the people in the photos doing on International Chocolate Day? Use these phrases.

| paint a picture | design a poster | present a report |
|---|---|---|
| make a milk shake | do research | eat candy bars |

**7** **Write.** What were you doing yesterday? Write true sentences.

1. At 7 a.m. I was taking the school bus ______.
2. At 9 a.m. ______.
3. At lunchtime ______

   when ______.
4. At 4:30 p.m. ______.
5. At 7 p.m. ______

   when ______.
6. At 8:30 p.m. ______.
7. At 10 p.m. ______

   when ______.

**8** **Work in a group.** Guess what everyone was doing yesterday. Take turns.

## 9 **Listen and repeat.** Then read and write. TR: A23

grams

mix

pour

recipe

ingredients

teaspoon

1. Learn how to make a delicious chocolate milk shake with this ____________________!
2. First, make sure you have all the ____________________: vanilla ice cream, milk, cocoa powder, and little pieces of dark chocolate.
3. Put 2 cups of vanilla ice cream, 1 cup of milk, and 6 ____________________ of cocoa powder into a blender. ____________________ the ingredients well.
4. When the liquid is ready, ____________________ the milk shake into two glasses. Decorate them with 30 ____________________ of dark chocolate. Enjoy!

## 10 **Work with a partner.** Stick the recipe in the correct order. Then listen to check your answers. TR: A24

I think "find the ingredients" is the first step.

I agree.

| 1 | 2 | 3 | 4 | 5 |
|---|---|---|---|---|
| | | | | |

## GRAMMAR TR: A25

| CAUSE | EFFECT |
|---|---|
| The boy **printed** out the recipe | **so that** he **could read** it while he was cooking. |
| We **put** all the ingredients on the table | **so that** it **would be** easy to find them later. |

**11** **Read and write.** Connect the cause and the effect.

1. Joseph Fry added new ingredients . . . (→ make a solid chocolate bar.)

   so that he could make a solid chocolate bar ______.

2. Sugar was mixed with chocolate . . . (→ taste sweeter.)

   ____________________.

3. Chocolate companies put caramel in chocolate . . . (→ have more variety.)

   ____________________.

4. A U.S. company printed a recipe . . . (→ people make chocolate at home.)

   ____________________.

5. Chocolate was ground and heated . . . (→ be smooth and melt.)

   ____________________.

**12** **Play a game.** Cut out the cards on page 161. Play with a partner. Ask and answer. Take turns.

**13** **Listen and read.** TR: A26

# The Story of Chocolate

The story of chocolate starts with the Olmecs and the Mayan people, who lived in the Americas more than 1,000 years ago. The Mayas have been growing cacao trees and using the seeds to make chocolate drinks for 2,000 years or more. In fact, scientists have analyzed chocolate residue from a ceramic "teapot." The results suggest that the Mayas were drinking chocolate as early as 2,600 years ago! Some artifacts show people pouring the liquid into cups. The Mayas also used the seeds as currency. With ten seeds they could buy a rabbit at the market.

The story continues with the Aztecs, who also loved chocolate and prepared it hot like the Mayas. But the Aztecs added spices so that it would taste better. Some rich people drank chocolate for breakfast, lunch, and dinner. Some were even buried with chocolate so that they could take it with them to the next world. Between 1200 and 1500 CE, the Aztecs also used chocolate as currency. In fact, by 1500, people were paying thirty seeds for a rabbit.

Let's continue our journey. When the Spanish arrived in the Aztec capital in 1519 CE, they tried chocolate and hated it. Without sugar it was extremely bitter, so the Spanish mixed it with sugar. In 1528 CE the Spanish took the Aztec seeds and recipe back to Spain so that they could drink chocolate there. Before this, no one in Europe knew about chocolate!

weird but true **People say that the Aztec ruler Moctezuma II drank 50 cups of chocolate a day.**

**14** **Complete the chart.** Write the cause or effect of each action.

| Cause | | Effect |
|---|---|---|
| 1. The Aztecs added another ingredient | → | |
| 2. | → | so that they could enjoy chocolate in their next life. |
| 3. The Spanish added sugar | → | |
| 4. | → | so that they could enjoy it in their own country. |

**15** **Read the text again.** Write how chocolate changed over time in these ways.

1. People: The Olmecs discovered it. Then the Mayas used it, followed by the Aztecs. Finally, the Spanish began to use chocolate.
2. Ingredients: ______
3. Chocolate as currency: ______

**16** **Work in a group of three.** Retell the story of chocolate. Take turns.

Temple of the Great Jaguar, Tikal, Guatemala

# Review

**1** **Listen to the phone call.** Check the things that Carlos has done. **TR: A27**

- ◯ learned to surf
- ◯ worn a life jacket
- ◯ fallen in the water a lot
- ◯ had an accident
- ◯ surfed skillfully
- ◯ been hang-gliding

**2** **Listen again.** Answer the questions. **TR: A28**

1. How long has Carlos been at the camp? for four days
2. How many times has he fallen in the water? ____________________
3. Is it raining today? ____________________
4. How many years has the teacher done extreme sports? ____________________
5. Why did he have to wear a life jacket and helmet yesterday? ____________________
____________________
6. Why did his friend show him how to climb rocks? ____________________
____________________

**3** **Work with a partner.** Discuss a vacation or camp that you enjoyed. Ask and answer questions. Use the words in the box.

| | |
|---|---|
| extremely | weather |
| incredibly | city or country |
| really | activities |
| so | place where you stayed |
| super | family |
| totally | friends |

I went on a hiking vacation in the mountains once. It was totally awesome.

Really? What was the weather like?

## 4 **Look at the pictures.** What were the boys and their sister doing at these times? Draw lines.

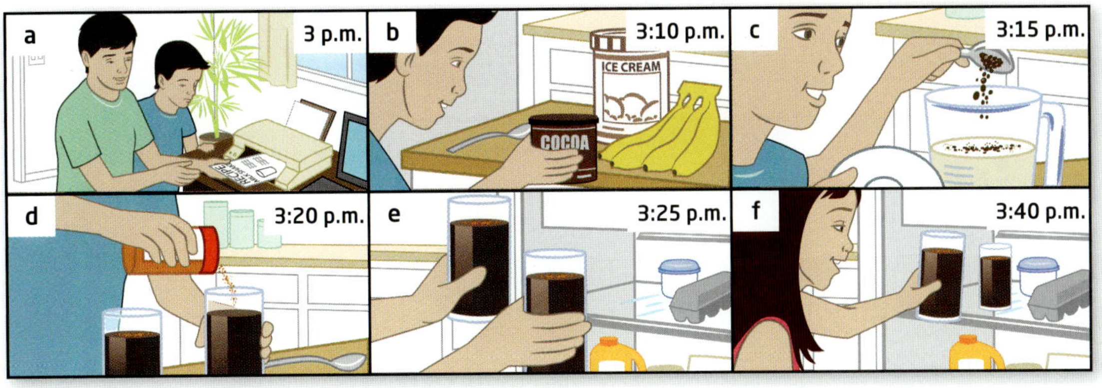


| | |
|---|---|
| 1. At 3 p.m. | a. Alex was putting the ingredients on the table. |
| 2. At 3:10 p.m. | b. they were storing the milk shake in the fridge because they were planning to drink it after their soccer game. |
| 3. At 3:15 p.m. | c. the boys' sister was taking their milk shake! |
| 4. At 3:20 p.m. | d. Daniel was printing the recipe. |
| 5. At 3:25 p.m. | e. the boys were putting cocoa powder into the blender. |
| 6. At 3:40 p.m. | f. they were pouring the liquid into glasses and putting cinnamon on top. |

## 5 **Work with a partner.** Look at the pictures. Tell the story. Add details.

## 6 **Work with a partner.** Ask and answer questions. Take notes.

1. Where / the Sphinx / build? Where was the Sphinx built?
2. When / the terra-cotta statues / make? ______
3. Where / the ruler Tutankhamun / buried? ______
4. Who / the first solid candy bar / invent / by? ______
5. Tutankhamun's treasures / excavate / by / archaeologists? ______
6. surfing / invent / in Hawaii? ______

## 7 **Listen to the answers.** Win a point for each correct answer! TR: A29

# Let's Talk

## I love it!

I will . . .
- start a conversation.
- change the topic.
- bring the topic back on track.
- discuss likes and dislikes.

**1 Listen and read.** TR: A30

Leo: Hey, **is everyone ready** for the camping trip?
Andres: Yes, I packed my backpack this morning.
Claudio: **By the way,** have you seen that new shark movie yet?
Andres: No, I haven't. **What's it like?**
Claudio: It's awesome. **I love it.**
Leo: I do, too. **Anyway,** let's talk about it later. **Back to** camping. Does anyone have a sleeping bag I can borrow?

| | | | |
|---|---|---|---|
| **Is everyone ready?**<br>Ready?<br>Let's start. | **By the way,** ___<br>Hey!<br>Before I forget, ___ | **What's it like?**<br>What's it about?<br>Is it good?<br><br>I like it. / **I love it.**<br>I hate it. / I can't stand it. | **Anyway,** ___<br>**Back to** ___<br>Look, ___ |

**2 Work in groups of three.** Have a conversation. Use the chart. Take turns. Change the subject to something else.

# Excuse me.

I will . . .
- ask for clarification.
- express doubt.
- interrupt politely.

## 3 Listen and read. TR: A31

Carla: **Hey, what did she say?**

Gabriel: **I think she said** we have to match the pictures and sentences, **but I'm not sure.**

Valeria: **I missed it, too.** Let's ask her.

Valeria: (to teacher) **Excuse me,** Ms. Trujillo. **Could you repeat that?**

Ms. Trujillo: **Sure. I'll go over it again.**

| **Hey, what did ________ say?**<br>I didn't catch that.<br>I missed that. | **I think she said ________, but I'm not sure.**<br>I'm not sure. **I missed it, too.**<br>Let's check. | **Excuse me, ________.**<br>I'm sorry, ________.<br>Could I ask a question, please? | **Could you repeat that?**<br>Could you say / explain that again? | **Sure.**<br>No problem!<br>Of course!<br>**I'll go over it again.**<br>I'll explain it again. |
|---|---|---|---|---|

## 4 Listen. You will hear two discussions. Circle the answers. TR: A32

1. What do the students think the teacher told them to do?
   a. practice a dialogue   b. write a dialogue   c. listen to a dialogue
2. Who didn't hear what the teacher said?
   a. the boy   b. the girl   c. the boy and the girl

## 5 Work in groups of three. Choose a situation and discuss.

1. Your teacher is telling you about a survey you are going to do. You didn't catch all the instructions.
2. Your teacher is going over the answers. You missed the last answer.
3. Your teacher is explaining tonight's homework. You didn't quite understand.

Unit 4

# Water, Water Everywhere

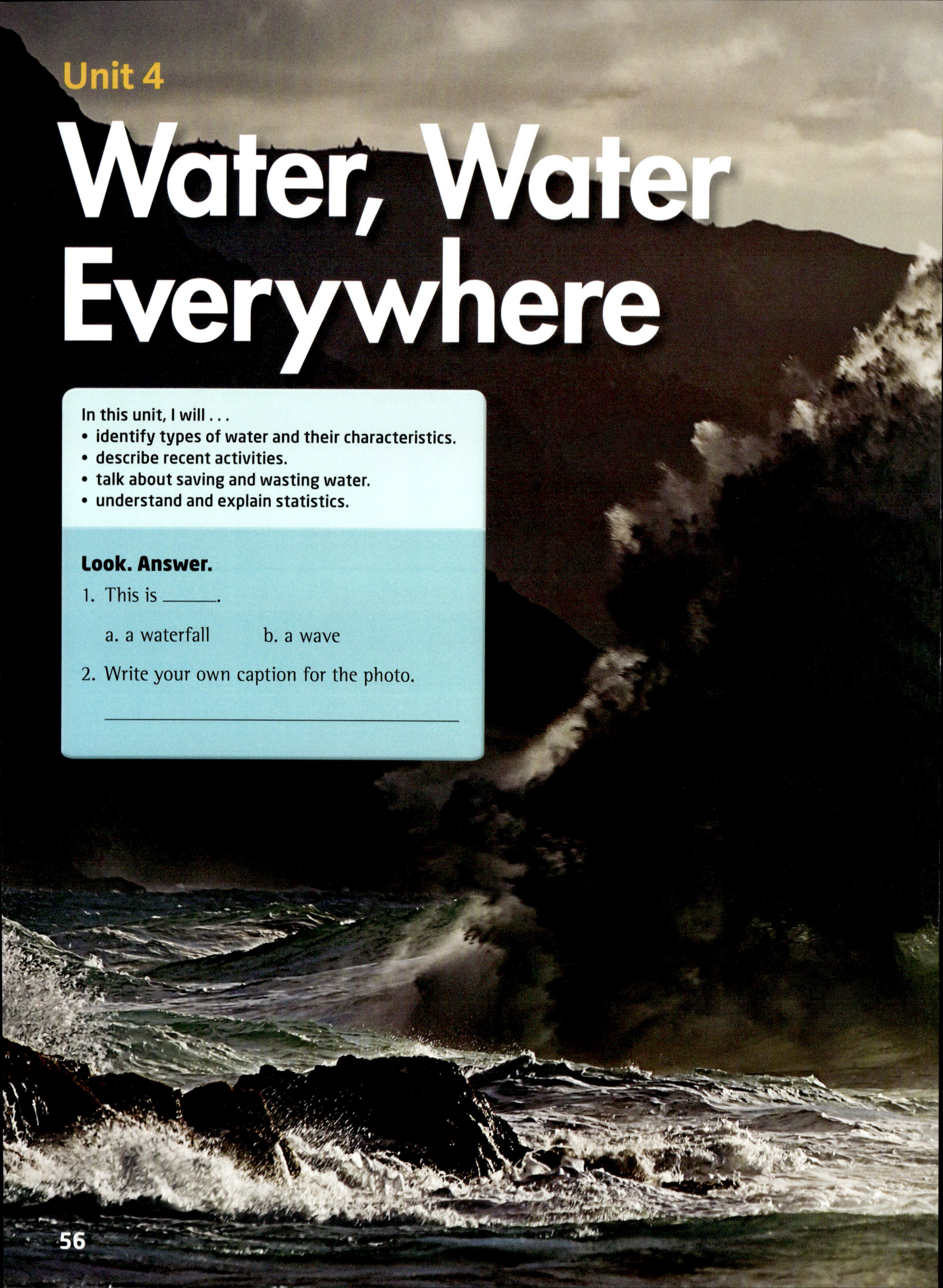

In this unit, I will . . .

- identify types of water and their characteristics.
- describe recent activities.
- talk about saving and wasting water.
- understand and explain statistics.

**Look. Answer.**

1. This is ______.

   a. a waterfall b. a wave

2. Write your own caption for the photo.

   ______________________________

Na Paili Coast, Kauai, Hawaii

## 4 Listen, read, and sing. TR: A35

# A World of Water

***A world of wonder. A world of water.***
***I've been thinking about***
***all the water in our world.***

***CHORUS***

*There's water in lakes, and water in the sea.*
*There's even water in you and me!*

*A puddle of water. A waterfall.*
*A tall glass of water. I love it all!*

*Fresh water, salt water, water in the sink.*
*I've been taking some time to think*
*about how much water there is in the world!*
*It's everywhere!*

***CHORUS***

*Fresh water, salt water, water in the sink.*
*I've been taking more time to think.*
*Why do we need water in this world?*

*We need water for crops and water for grass.*
*We need water for plants and animals, too!*

*Everything needs water.*
*Everything needs water.*
*I know that's true!*

***CHORUS***

*A world of wonder. A world of water.*
*Have you been thinking about*
*all the water in our world?*

## 5 Answer the questions.

1. Circle four things that need water.
2. Is there water inside you? Yes No
3. Invent a new title for the song!

_______________________________

Iguazu Falls, on the border of Argentina and Brazil

## GRAMMAR TR: A36

How long **have** you and your sister **been taking** swimming lessons?

I**'ve been taking** swimming lessons **for** three months.
**for** about a year.

My sister **has been taking** swimming lessons **since** March.
**since** she was nine.

## 6 **Read and write.** Complete the sentences.

play soak surf take water

1. It has been raining since three o'clock. It's really wet outside now.
2. My brother ______________ water polo for three years.
3. I ______________ in the bathtub for half an hour. It feels so good!
4. Mom and Dad ______________ the plants in the yard for fifteen minutes.
5. My sister ______________ a shower for nearly thirty minutes. She takes forever!
6. You're a good surfer. How long ______________ you ______________?

**7** **What about you?** Imagine you are visiting three of these places. On a sheet of paper, write at least *three* things that you have been doing at each place. Don't tell the name of the place!

The Dead Sea
The Asmat Swamp
The Hubbard Glacier
The Pyramids
Qin Shi Huang Di's tomb

*I've been counting statues.*

**8** **Work in a group.** Listen to each other's sentences. Guess where people are. Take turns.

## 9 **Listen and repeat.** Look at the pictures. Complete the sentences. **TR: A37**

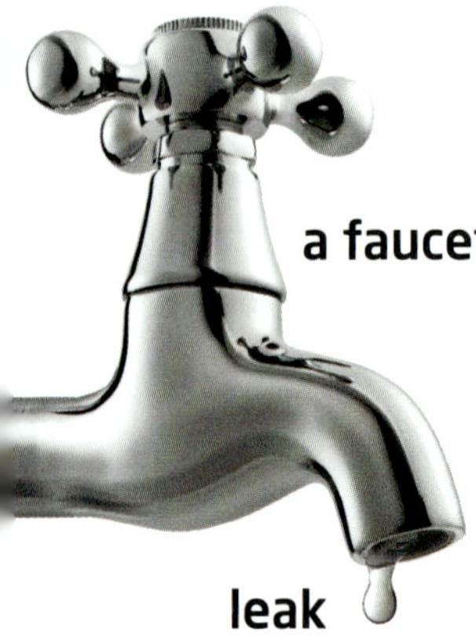

a faucet

leak

a drain

save

waste

1. There are many ways you can ______________________ water at home. For example, you can take a shower instead of a bath. Showers use less water.
2. If the dishwasher isn't full when you use it, you'll ______________________ water.
3. Use the handle to turn off the ______________________ while you brush your teeth. Turn it on again when you need it.
4. Faucets that ______________________ waste a lot of fresh water. If you see drops of water coming from a faucet, tell someone.
5. Don't throw trash down the ______________________.
6. When we went camping, we didn't have ______________________.

## 10 **Listen and stick.** Work with a partner. Compare your answers. **TR: A38**

If you leave the water running, you waste 11 liters per minute!

That's right! We should turn off the faucet when we brush our teeth.

| 11 liters | 15 liters | 40 liters | 75 liters | 230 liters | 265 liter |
|---|---|---|---|---|---|
| | | | | | |

## GRAMMAR TR: A39

Do **whatever** you can to save water.
Save fresh water **whenever** you can and **wherever** you go.
**Whoever** threw paint down the drain is in trouble!

**11** **Read.** Complete the sentences.

1. ____________________ people throw trash down a storm drain, they pollute water.
2. ____________________ told the teacher about that leaking faucet saved water.
3. People use 265 liters of water ____________________ they take a bath.
4. ____________________ glaciers are found, the average yearly temperature is below freezing.
5. ____________________ you leave the faucet running while you brush your teeth, you waste 11 liters of water every minute.
6. People should do ____________________ they can to protect the oceans.

**12** **Play a game.** Cut out the board game on page 163. Play the game in a small group.

## 13 Listen and read. TR: A40

# A World of Water

Nearly 75% of the earth is covered by water. There is water above ground called *surface water*, such as lakes, swamps, and rivers, and water that's under the ground called *groundwater*. Water even exists in the sky! That is called *water vapor*. There is water everywhere.

Although we have a lot of water, we can't drink most of it. 97.5% of the earth's water is salt water, which humans can't drink. The rest is fresh water, which we can drink. However, we can't use most of our drinking water because 70% is frozen—like the Hubbard Glacier. Also, we can only reach 30% of our groundwater, and most of that is polluted. In fact, we can only drink about 1% of the world's fresh water.

We don't drink most of our fresh water. Only 5% goes to the faucets in our homes. About 95% is used to produce food, clothes, and energy. We don't see that water, but it is a big part of our "water footprint," or the total amount of water we use. For example, we don't see the water that was used to make a T-shirt. We only see the T-shirt. But 2,700 liters (713 gallons) of water were used to produce it!

Earth has always had the same amount of water. However, there are more people on the planet now, and we all need water. If we want water in the future, we must not waste it or pollute it now!

**weird but true**

**3 liters of water are used to produce a 1-liter bottle of water.**

**The World's Water Resources**

Iguazu Falls

## 14 **Read.** Complete the definitions.

1. Water in lakes, rivers, and swamps is called ________________.
2. Water in the clouds or sky is referred to as ________________.
3. Water that is underground is called ________________.
4. The water we can drink is called ________________.

## 15 **Read.** Label the graphs.

**Where does our fresh water go?**

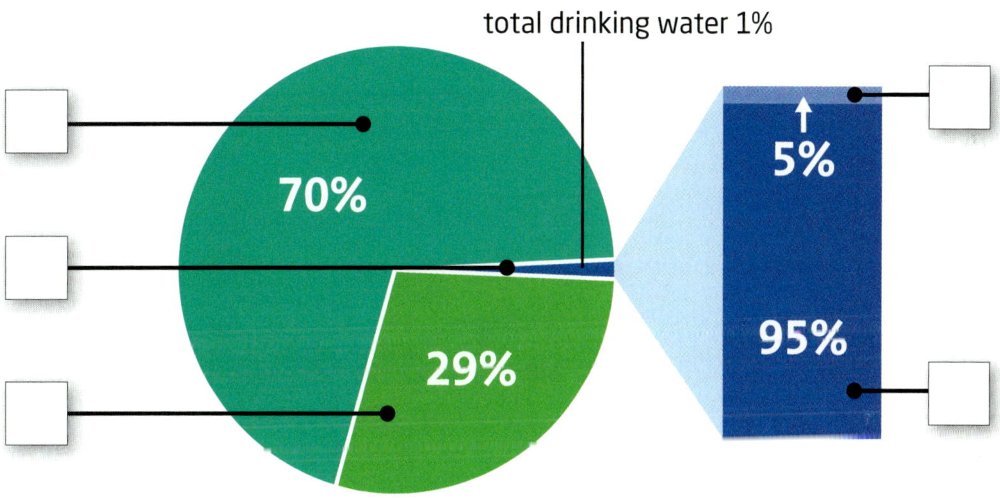


1. To our homes
2. Frozen
3. To produce food, clothes, and energy
4. Polluted groundwater
5. In clean places that we can reach

## 16 **Work with a partner.** Discuss the information in the graphs.

## Paragraphs of Information

When you write a paragraph of information, you should state facts and statistics and give examples.

**17** **Read.** Read the paragraph of information. Underline the statistics.

### Save water outdoors!

About 5 percent of the world's fresh water goes to our homes for drinking, cooking, and cleaning. The average family uses one quarter of their fresh water in the yard! In many countries, people waste 50 to 80 percent of their yard water because they water grass when it's hot outside! People should water early in the morning or late in the afternoon when there is less sun. People also waste 10 to 35 liters of water every time they leave a hose running for one minute. But why do we use our drinking water on grass? We could collect rainwater to water the plants!

People wash their cars with our drinking water, too! When people wash their cars at home, 50 percent of the chemicals from car soap go down the drains and flow to freshwater rivers. Today, about 40 percent of our rivers are polluted. Remind your family and friends where the water goes. You can make a difference!

**18** **Write.** Write a paragraph of information. Describe ways to save water inside your home. Give examples. Remember to include facts and statistics.

**19** **Work in a small group.** Share your ideas.

NATIONAL GEOGRAPHIC

# Mission

## Conserve water at school.

- Work in a small group. Discuss how water is used in your school every day, such as in the classrooms, bathrooms, cafeteria, and at sports facilities. Where do you think most water is used?
- How can you help save water in your school? Think of ideas. Discuss and write the best ideas below.

______________________________

______________________________

______________________________

______________________________

______________________________

- Work with another group. Share your ideas. Are they the same or different? Which ideas does everyone like best?

*"I just want to do my part to be sure we humans conserve water and share it with all of life."*

**Sandra Postel**
**Fresh Water Conservationist**
National Geographic Fellow

## 20 Make a world map of water.

1. Work in a group of three.
2. Research two bodies of water in the world, such as rivers, lakes, oceans, or waterfalls.
3. Write a short summary about each body of water.
4. Print or find a world map. Stick each summary at the location of the body of water.
5. Add photos and pictures to your map.

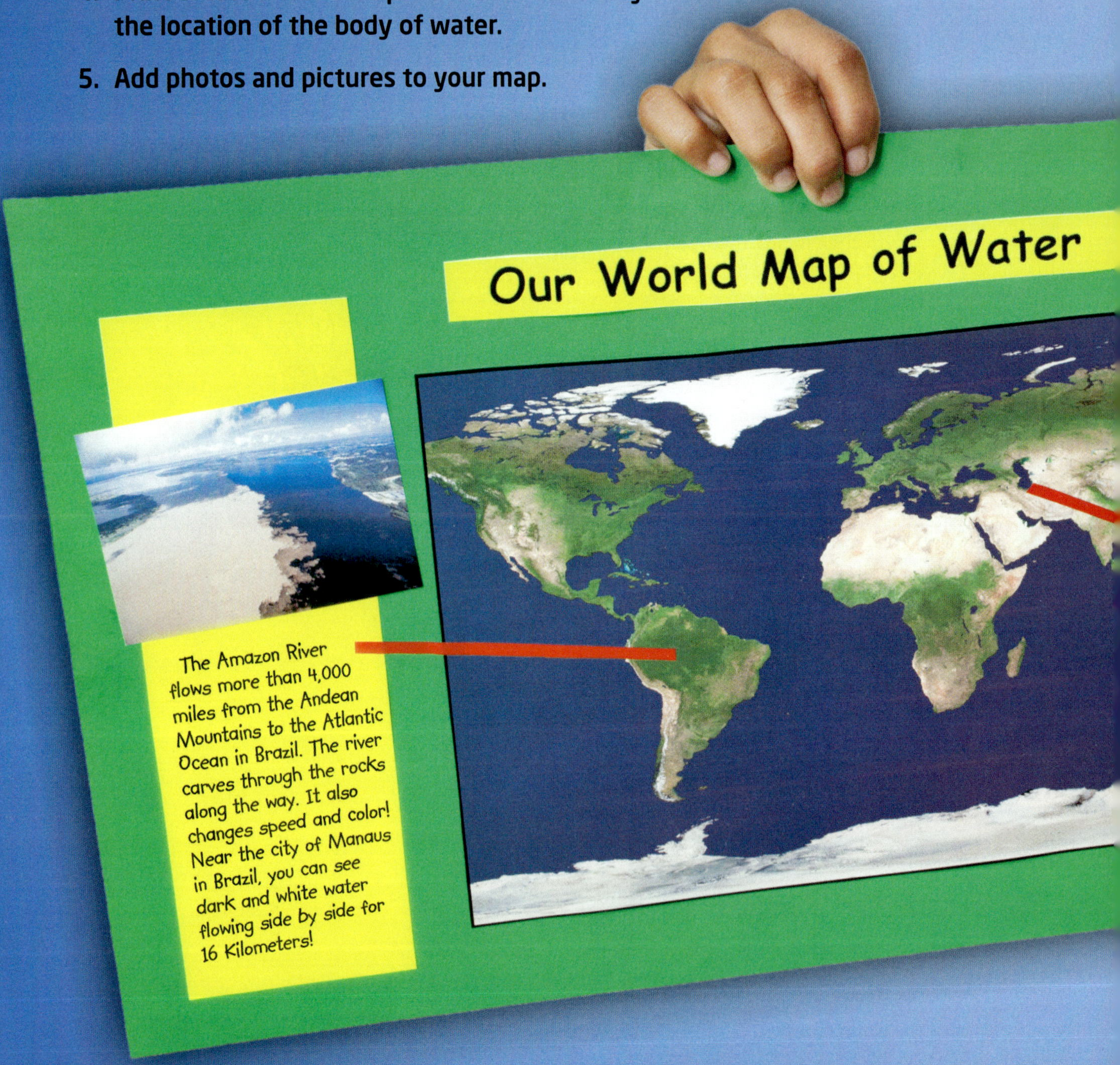

The Caspian Sea is the largest lake in the world.

## Now I can . . .

- ◯ identify types of water and their characteristics.
- ◯ describe recent activities.
- ◯ talk about saving and wasting water.
- ◯ understand and explain statistics.

Unit 5

# It's a Small World

In this unit, I will . . .

- identify small creatures and their characteristics.
- describe creatures.
- report what other people say.
- write a science report.

**Look and talk.**

1. Describe this creature in one word.
2. Where does this creature live?
3. What do you think it is?

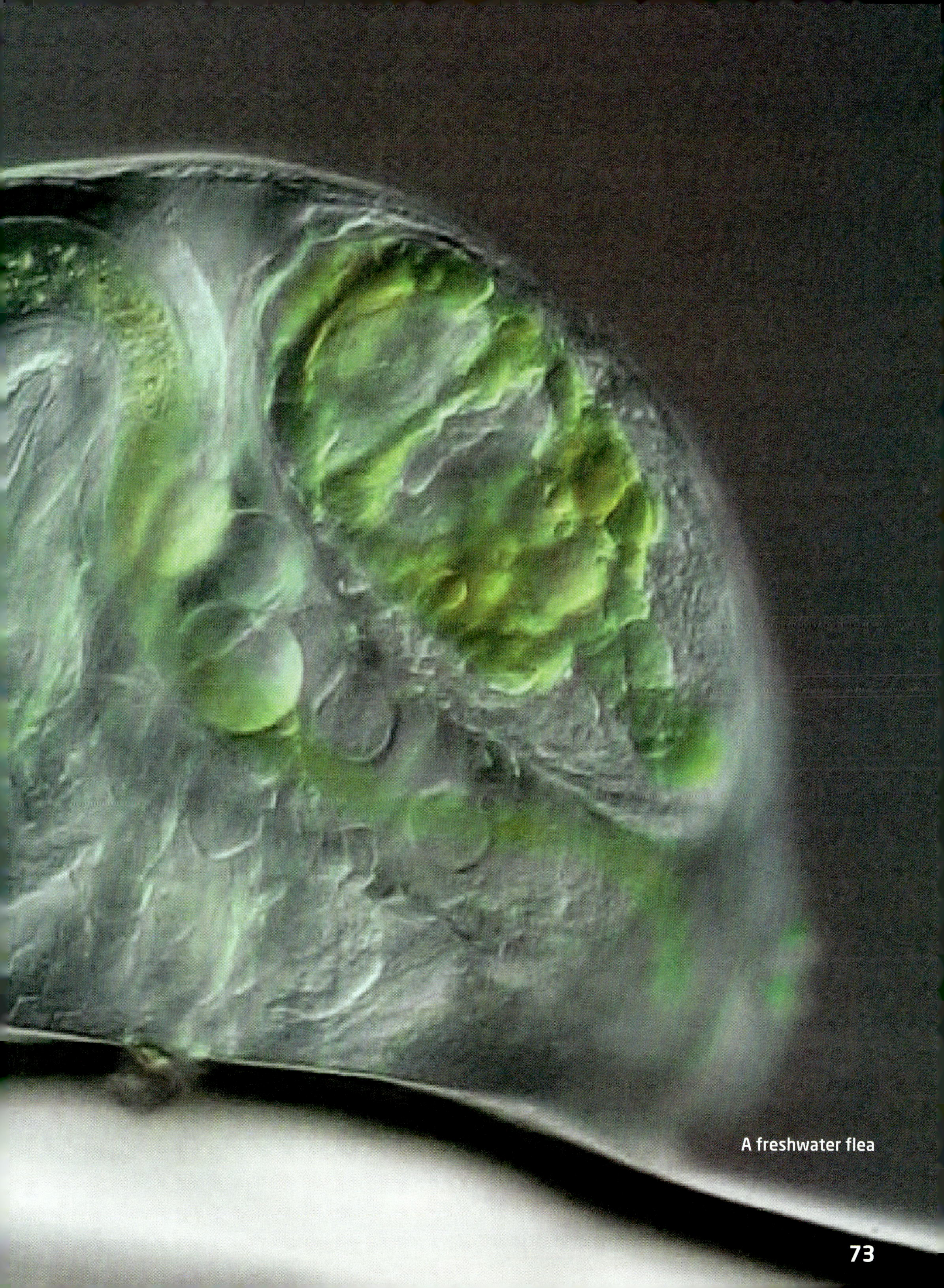

A freshwater flea

## 1 Listen and read. TR: A41

## 2 Listen and repeat. TR: A42

We share our planet with millions of small creatures: cool spiders, beautiful striped butterflies, ugly bugs, cute hamsters, and fascinating fish. Can you think of more little creatures that live on Earth?

Eyelash mites are 0.3 millimeters long. You can only see them through a **microscope.** They look **horrible,** but they're very **common.**

**Habitat:** our eyelashes

Characteristics: These **organisms** eat dead skin **cells.** They crawl around our skin at night.

This seahorse is an orange fish that's just sixteen **millimeters** long. It's smaller than a **human's** tooth and has a long **thin** tail.

Habitat: warm water, near coral

Characteristics: It uses camouflage. It **grabs** food that floats by. Male seahorses have babies.

The **male** bee hummingbird is the smallest bird in the world. (It's about five and a half **centimeters** long.) The **female** is bigger. Its eggs are smaller than coffee beans.

Habitat: near flowers

Characteristic: It can move its strong wings eighty times a second.

**3** **Work with a partner.** What did you learn? Ask and answer.

## 4 Listen, read, and sing. TR: A43

# Look into a Microscope

***Look into a microscope.***
***Tell me what you see.***
***There's a tiny world in front of us,***
***full of tiny things to see.***

*Let's take a look.*

*My teacher said that creatures*
*smaller than a human hair*
*live in our world.*
*She said we'd find them everywhere!*

*Wow!*

*Some look like strange monsters,*
*with jaws and claws and horrible eyes.*
*But don't forget how small they are.*
*Don't forget their size.*

***CHORUS***

*Look a little closer!*

*There are tiny habitats*
*where predator and prey*
*have tiny little battles*
*every minute of the day.*

*Wow!*

*Mites live on our eyelashes!*
*That's just the way it goes.*
*What do they eat for breakfast?*
*Do you really want to know?*

***CHORUS***

*There's a tiny world in front of us,*
*full of tiny things to see.*

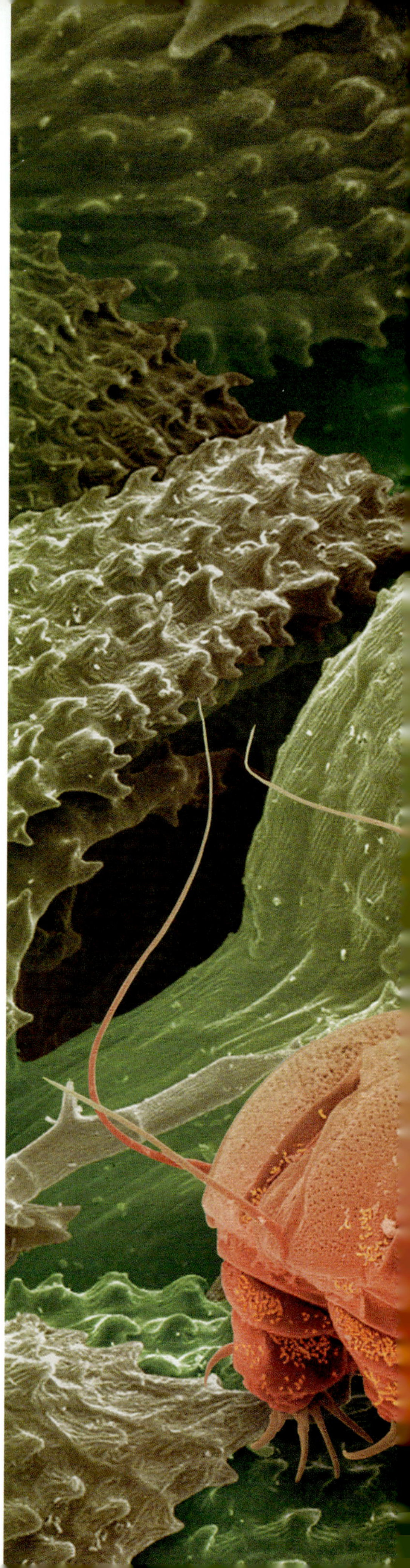

## 5 Check T for *True* and F for *False*.

1. Tiny creatures are everywhere. (T) (F)
2. Some creatures live on our jaws. (T) (F)
3. Small creatures never eat breakfast. (T) (F)

Water bears

## GRAMMAR TR: A44

| | | |
|---|---|---|
| Dad: "This sea horse **lives** near coral." | → | My dad said that this sea horse **lived** near coral. |
| Mom: "Eyelash mites **don't have** wings." | → | My mom said that eyelash mites **didn't have** wings. |
| Teacher: "Hummingbirds **can't** smell." | → | Our teacher said that hummingbirds **couldn't** smell. |
| Ben: "You **are** wrong." | → | Ben said that I **was** wrong. |

**6** **Read.** Report what your teacher told you. Write the reported sentences in your notebook.

1. "An organism is a living thing. It can be a plant or an animal."
2. "Most organisms have more than one cell."
3. "The Denise seahorse isn't very common."
4. "The hummingbird lives near flowers, but it can't smell them."
5. "You can see an eyelash mite through a microscope."
6. "I don't like things that crawl on my head."

**7** **What do you know?** Work with a partner. Tell one fact about each creature. Use the prompts to help you. Your partner reports on what you said. Take turns.

female - male
eggs - beans
can move - wings

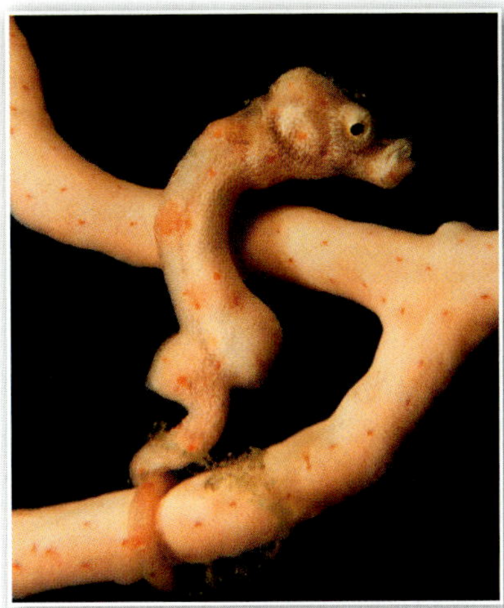

smaller - human's tooth
live - coral
male - babies

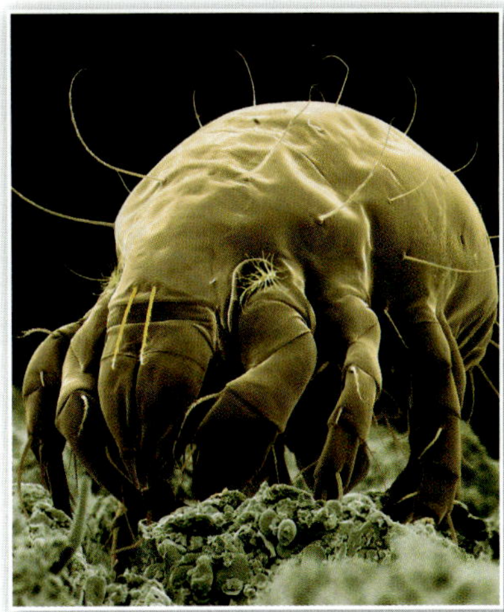

0.3 millimeters long
crawl - skin
eat - skin cell

**8** **Work in a group.** Write two true sentences and one false sentence. Read them to the group. Take turns.

## 9 **Listen and repeat.** Look at the photos. Match. Complete the sentences. **TR: A45**

b. tiny

d. furry

e. strange

f. spotted

__a__ 1. That's so cute. Look at how the ____________ elephant is standing over the baby!

____ 2. The ____________ lizard is sitting on a finger. It's so small!

____ 3. The lizard has a long ____________ tail.

____ 4. Do you see the ____________ ladybug on the blade of grass?

____ 5. That little ____________ monkey is beautiful.

____ 6. Look at that ____________ creature in the water. Where is its head?

## 10 **Work with a partner.** Talk and stick. Take turns.

This animal is soft and furry.

It's a rabbit!

| 1 | 2 | 3 | 4 | 5 |
|---|---|---|---|---|

## GRAMMAR TR: A46

| Opinion | Size | Age | Shape | Color | Pattern | Origin | Material | Thing |
|---|---|---|---|---|---|---|---|---|
| cute | | young | | | striped | | furry | creatures |
| | tiny | | pointed | gray | | | | ears |
| strange | | | | black | | Australian | hairy | spiders |
| common | | adult | | | spotted | | | bugs |

**11** **Read and write.** Describe the creatures.

1. These cute gray furry animals are called marmosets.
   (furry / gray / cute)
2. The insect with the ______________ antennae is a firefly.
   (pointed / long / black)
3. This ______________ frog changes color when it is scared.
   (adult / tiny / amazing)
4. The ladybug is a ______________ bug.
   (spotted / red and black / common)
5. The Denise seahorse has a ______________ head.
   (pointed / strange / orange)
6. These eyelash mites are very ______________ creatures.
   (transparent / tiny / ugly)

**12** **Play a game.** Cut out the game board and pictures on page 165. Choose eight of them for your game board. Listen and play bingo. TR: A47

## 13 Listen and read. TR: A48

There are about 1.5 million species on Earth, but how many do you see every day? You often see the big colorful animals, like birds, mammals, and fish. But look more closely. Can you see the tiny creatures, too? Insects make up 80 percent of the world's species. Look on the ground. Imagine you could look under the ground, too. Many organisms with one cell live there. Life is everywhere around us, in every cubic foot.

David Liittschwager is a photographer who wanted to find out how many creatures existed in one cubic foot. So he made a 12-inch cube with a green metal frame and put it in five habitats. He chose a tropical rainforest (Costa Rica), a coral reef (Pacific Ocean), the Table Mountain (South Africa), a freshwater river (USA), and a city park (New York). Three weeks were spent at each site. He observed, counted, and took photos of everything—down to 1 millimeter in size—that crawled or flew into the cube.

The results were amazing. Liittschwager found both common and rare creatures. He also discovered many new species, like a strange transparent octopus that is the size of a fingernail! In total, more than a thousand different organisms were photographed and analyzed. Liittschwager said the One Cubic Foot experience was like "finding treasure." Although the coral reef had the widest range of biodiversity, all the other habitats were full of life. Even the city park!

**transparent octopus**

**1 foot (ft.) =**

**12 inches (in.)**
**0.3048 meters (m)**
**30.48 centimeters (cm)**

**14** **Read and write.** Underline the best title for the text. Write it in the title box.

A Biography of David Liittschwager

Life Is Everywhere

How to Do a "One Cubic Foot" Project

**15** **Read.** Match each word or phrase with its correct meaning.

| | |
|---|---|
| 1. one cubic foot | a. to watch |
| 2. rare | b. a place where living and nonliving things exist together |
| 3. biodiversity | c. 12 inches x 12 inches x 12 inches |
| 4. an ecosystem | d. the variety of life on Earth |
| 5. to observe | e. not common |

**16** **Work with a partner.** Read the text again. Ask and answer questions. Use the answers in the cube.

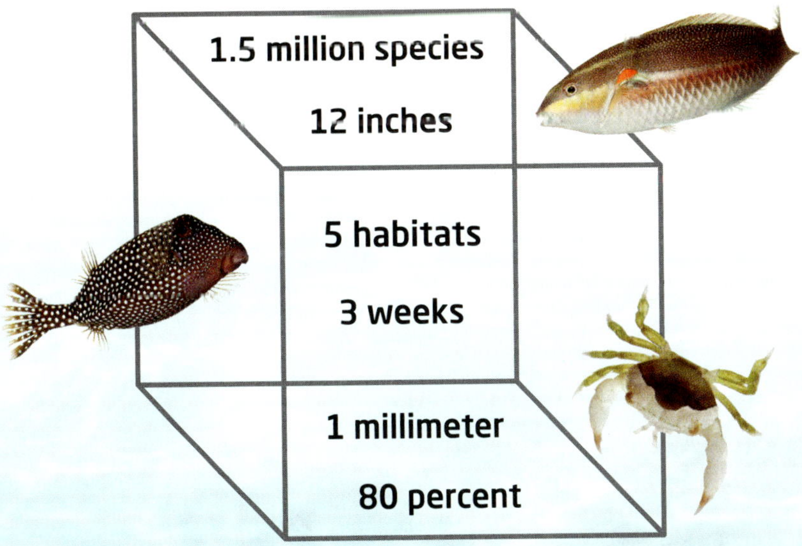


**weird but true**

**There are more organisms in one tablespoon of soil than there are people on Earth.**

## Science Reports

When you write a science report, include statistics and details. For example, if you are writing about an animal, include its scientific name, information about its habitat, food and other characteristics, as well as expert opinions. You can also use words that describe size, shape, color, pattern, and origin.

**17** **Read.** Read the report. Number the order in which you find the information on the list below (1-6).

| | |
|---|---|
| ___ food | 1 scientific name |
| ___ an interesting fact | ___ habitat |
| ___ conclusion | ___ physical characteristics |

### An Interesting Sea Creature

Denise's pygmy seahorse (scientific name: Hippocampus denise) is a species of fish that is found in Asia. The natural habitat of H. denise is coral reefs, where it uses camouflage to hide. H. denise eats soft coral and is found at a depth of 13–90 m.

H. denise is light orange in color, with a strange head that resembles a horse and a long, thin, pointed tail. It grows to a total length of 16 millimeters (about 0.6 inches). According to the Australian biologist Rudie Kuiter, it is so small that it can escape from predators.

An interesting characteristic of the Denise seahorses is that males have the babies, not females. Males can carry 10–1,000 babies during their lives. Because the Denise seahorse uses camouflage to hide and lives so deep in the corals, scientists hope it is safe from problems other seahorses face.

**18** **Write.** Write an animal report. Include statistics, facts, and an expert opinion. Remember to use descriptive words.

**19** **Work in a small group.** Share your writing.

NATIONAL GEOGRAPHIC

# Mission

## Be curious.

- Scientists have recently discovered this new species, the mouse lemur. Work in a small group. Make a list of things you would like to know about this animal. Discuss.
- How could you find the answers to your questions? Discuss and write your best ideas in the box.

*"The more questions I asked the more it became clear to me that much about our natural world still remained a mystery."*

**Mireya Mayor**
**Primatologist/Conservationist**
Emerging Explorer

- Work with another group. Share your ideas. Are they the same or different? Which ideas does everyone like best?

## 20 Research two related animals.

1. Choose two related animals: one large and one small. For example, you might choose a tiger and a cat.
2. Research the two animals.
3. Make a poster about the two animals.
   a. Write a short summary about the animals. What do they have in common? How are they different?
   b. Add photos, pictures, and a map showing where the animals live.

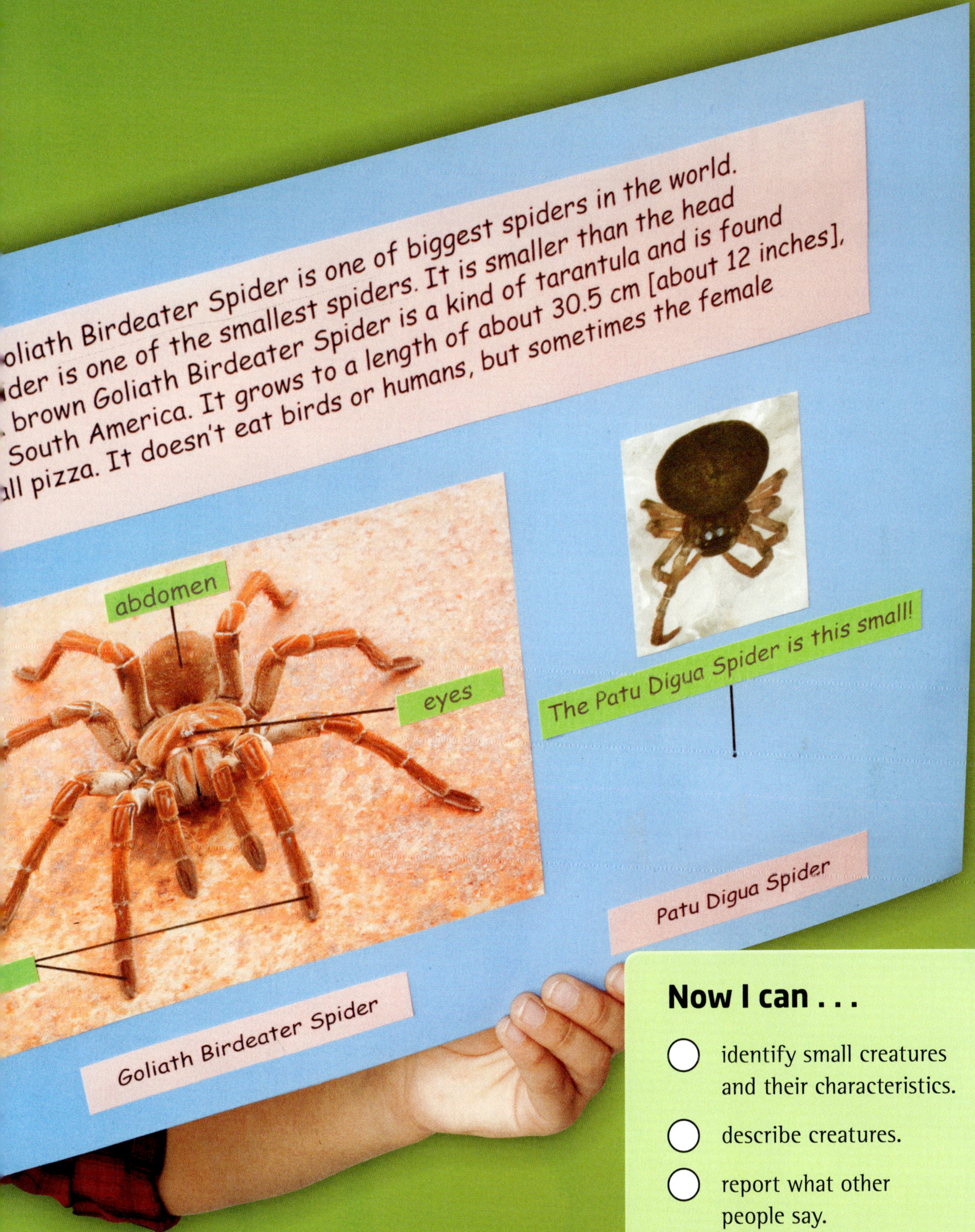


## Now I can . . .

- ○ identify small creatures and their characteristics.
- ○ describe creatures.
- ○ report what other people say.
- ○ write a science report.

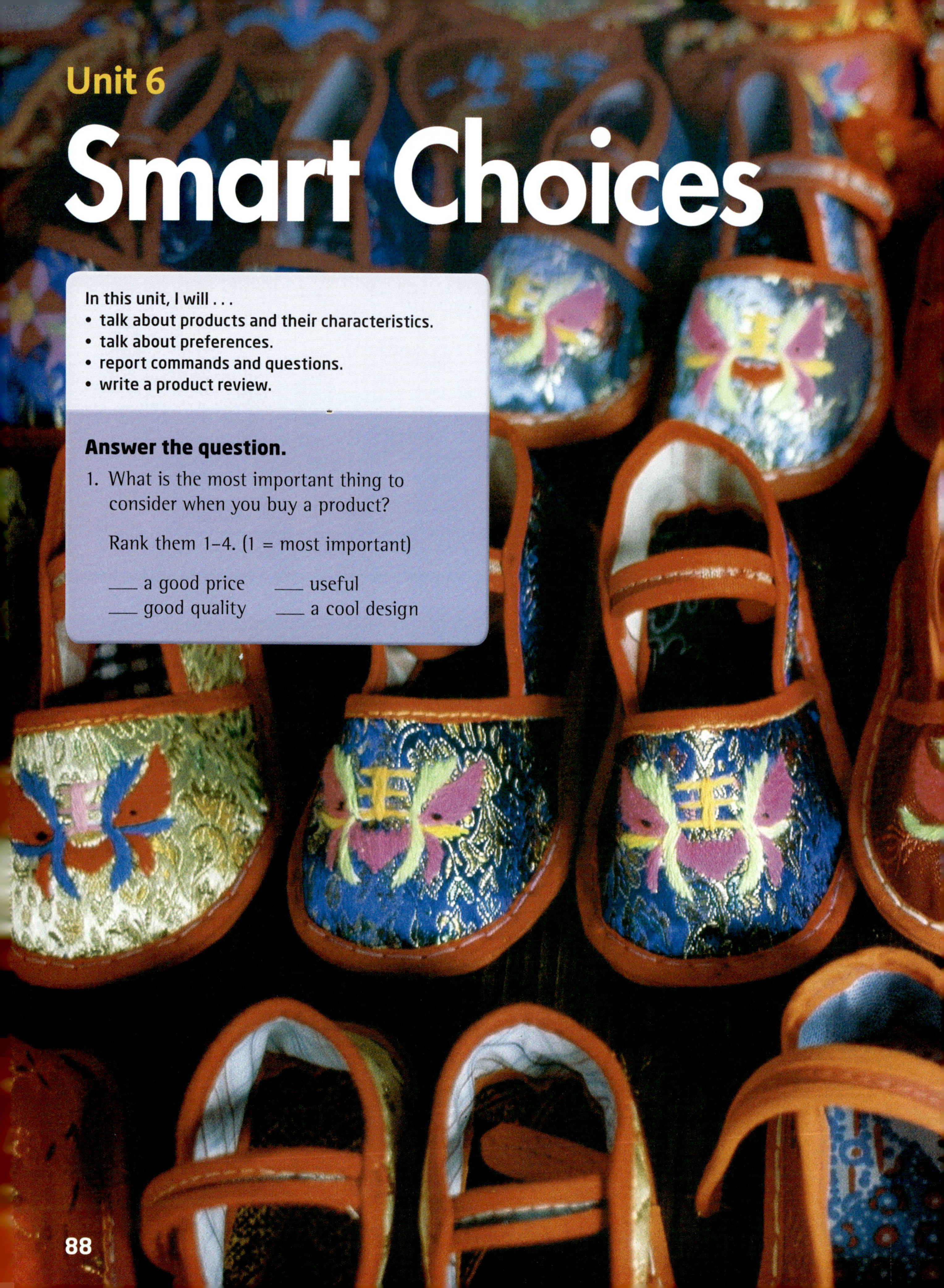

Unit 6

# Smart Choices

In this unit, I will . . .

- talk about products and their characteristics.
- talk about preferences.
- report commands and questions.
- write a product review.

**Answer the question.**

1. What is the most important thing to consider when you buy a product?

   Rank them 1–4. (1 = most important)

   ___ a good price ___ useful
   ___ good quality ___ a cool design

**1** **Listen and read.** TR: B2

**2** **Listen and repeat.** TR: B3

Have you ever bought a **product** that **broke** the next day? It's not fair, especially if it **cost** a lot of money! It's also bad for the **manufacturer.** Unhappy **customers** tell many people if a product does not have good **quality!**

Most manufacturers **test** their products carefully before selling them. Cars must pass **safety** tests. To test a car, they put **dummies,** which look like humans, inside the car. Then they make the car crash. **Crash tests** show manufacturers what happens on **impact.**

Toys are tested, too. The “torque test” twists toys until they break. The “drop test” **drops** toys on the floor! **Waterproof** toys are **dipped** in water. Machines **tear** balloons. If something doesn’t work, manufacturers must **fix** the problem.

**3** **Work with a partner.** What did you learn? Ask and answer.

## 4 Listen, read, and sing. TR: B4

# Safe Buys

***Many of the things we buy***
***are tested for safety.***
***That's good! Products should be safe.***
***They should be safe for you and me.***

*When you're a customer,*
*the products you buy shouldn't break.*
*A manufacturer*
*should try not to make mistakes.*

*Is this clock waterproof?*
*It goes tick tock.*
*Let's dip the clock.*
*It's just a test to make sure everything is safe.*

***CHORUS***

*Quality is important.*
*Products should be safe.*
*A factory that makes things*
*should test everything, just in case.*

*A dummy sits inside a car.*
*The car speeds up!*
*BAM!! It's a crash!*
*It's just a test to make sure everything is safe.*

***CHORUS***

*Safe for you and me!*

## 5 Complete the sentences. Answer.

1a. The two products tested in the song are a clock and ____________________.

1b. We test products so that they are ____________________ for people.

2. Have you ever bought anything that broke? What happened?

## GRAMMAR TR: B5

| | |
|---|---|
| "**Put** your pen in your backpack." | Mom told me **to put** my pen in my backpack. |
| "**Don't break** my toys." | My brother told me **not to break** his toys. |

**6** **Read.** Your friends lent you a toy. Write their instructions about the toy. Circle the toy.

1. "Look after it." *They told me to look after it.*
2. "Don't drop it." ______________________
3. "Don't tear its clothes." ______________________
4. "Don't twist its arms." ______________________
5. "Enjoy it." ______________________

**7** **What about you?** Imagine your friends want to use some of your things. Tell them what to do and what not to do.

Your backpack

1. ______________________________

2. ______________________________

3. ______________________________

Your new pen

1. ______________________________

2. ______________________________

3. ______________________________

Your bicycle

1. ______________________________

2. ______________________________

3. ______________________________

**8** **Work in a group.** Compare your ideas. Are they the same or different?

## 9 **Listen and repeat.** Read and complete the paragraph. TR: B6

This is a great cell phone for young people who only need to make phone calls and send ______________________. It doesn't have ______________________, so you can't send e-mails. The phone has a cool design and comes in many colors. Also, it will survive lots of ______________________. Tests show that it doesn't break if you drop it. The screen is large, and the ______________________ are easy to press. The ______________________ is good in most places. Young people might prefer a cell phone that comes with games and other ______________________, but this is a great simple phone.

## 10 **Work with a partner.**

Listen and stick.
Compare your answers. TR: B7

How do manufacturers test the keys?

They press them thousands of times for five days.

Yes, I have the same answer.

| 1 | 2 | 3 | 4 | 5 |
|---|---|---|---|---|
| | | | | |

## GRAMMAR TR: B8

| | |
|---|---|
| Lisa: "**What** do I need to do next?" | Lisa asked me **what** she **needed** to do next. |
| Ken: "**Can** you help me?" | Ken asked me **if** I **could** help him. |

**11** **Read.** Look at the pictures. Follow the model. Write in your notebook.

1. The woman asked him if she could help him.

**12** **Play a memory game.** Cut out the cards on page 167. Play in a small group.

## 13 Listen and read. TR: B9

# Be an Ad Detective!

Every day we see ads—on TV, in magazines, on websites, in the street, and on our computer screens. We hear them, too. But often we don't notice them. A famous film producer once showed over one hundred products in his movie, but most people didn't notice them!

Are you an ad detective? Can you understand the messages advertisers send you? To be an ad detective, it is useful to know how ads work. Let's look at some typical advertising techniques.

1. **Group pressure:** An ad shows lots of young people, each with their own cell phone. Message: Everyone has a cell phone. You need one, too!
2. **Association:** Everyone looks happy and healthy in the ad. They're cool and beautiful, too. Message: If you buy the product, you will be happy and cool like these people.
3. **Testimonials:** A famous athlete says he wears a certain brand of sneakers. Message: You'll be good at sports, too, if you buy these sneakers. Or, because a famous athlete wears these sneakers, they're a product you can trust.
4. **Repetition:** These ads mention the product many times and say wonderful things about it. Message: You need to remember the product.
5. **Time pressure:** These ads use expressions like "Buy now! Half price this week." Message: You should buy the product quickly before you miss a great opportunity.

Ads are interesting, but you can make better decisions about what to buy when you know these techniques! Try these tips: read product reviews, compare products, test products in the store, and, if you are not sure, wait 24 hours before buying. You may decide that you don't really need or want the product!

**14** **Read.** Reread the text. Find the technique used in each ad below. Write the number.

a. ___3___ A popular hip-hop singer is advertising some clothes.

b. ______ Summer vacations end next week. Backpacks are half price this week.

c. ______ You hear the name of the product seven times in a thirty-second ad.

d. ______ Some friends are playing outdoors. They're all wearing the same sneakers.

e. ______ Young people are cycling outdoors. They're laughing. The sun is shining.

**15** **Read the text again.** Find other word forms.

1. advertising → ___ad___
2. decide → ______
3. producer → ______
4. repeat → ______

**16** **Work with a partner.** Look at the tips in the last paragraph. Discuss. Which is:

1. the most useful tip?
2. a tip you already use?
3. a tip you would never use?
4. a tip you would like to try?

**Weird but true** The time shown on most watches in ads is 10:10. This is because the hands of the watch in this position look like a smiling face.

## Product Reviews

In a product review, you help the customer decide what to buy. It is not an ad, so you can describe both the positive and negative aspects of the product. To emphasize the good points, use expressions like *above all, particularly, of course, in fact, really, the truth is,* and *in addition.*

**17** **Read.** Read the review. Underline the expressions that the writer uses to emphasize the positive features of the backpack.

### Carry Your Books in Style

This is a good quality backpack for school kids aged eleven to thirteen who need to carry a lot of books. It is made of strong material that will survive a lot of wear and tear. In fact, we tested it and it doesn't tear easily. In addition, the material is waterproof, so kids' books won't get wet in the rain.

We particularly like this backpack because it doesn't weigh a lot. Of course, leather backpacks may look cooler, but they are heavier. Carrying a heavy backpack is bad for your back, so the truth is, we prefer this one.

Above all, we like that the backpack comes in many colors and designs. The only problem? The straps are a little short. So we suggest that you try it on in the store before you decide. We give this backpack four stars.****

**18** **Write.** Review a product. Write about why you like it and make a recommendation. Use expressions of emphasis for the good points.

**19** **Share your work with a small group.** Listen and take notes.

| Name | Product | Good points | Bad points | Number of stars |
|---|---|---|---|---|
| | | | | |
| | | | | |

NATIONAL GEOGRAPHIC

# Mission

## Be aware of why you are making decisions.

*"Socially contagious behavior is common in humans."*

**Iain Couzin**
**Behavioral Ecologist**
Emerging Explorer

- **Work in a small group. Think of the things you own. Why did you or your parent buy them? How did you feel when you bought them? How did you feel a month later?**
- **Have you ever bought something just because your friends have it? Why? Write some examples.**

- **Work with another group. Share your examples. Are they the same or different? Which product was a good idea to buy? Which one was a bad idea? Discuss why.**

## 20 Make a collage of ads.

1. Choose a product. Cut out advertisements that sell your product.
2. Analyze the ads.
   a. Who is responsible for the ad? What are they advertising?
   b. Who is the advertiser selling the product to?
   c. What techniques does the ad use?
   d. What does the ad say or suggest about the product?
3. Make a collage using the ads.

## Now I can . . .

- ◯ talk about products and their characteristics.
- ◯ talk about preferences.
- ◯ report commands and questions.
- ◯ write a product review.

# Review

**1** **Listen.** What kind of cell phone has Olga bought? Check the features. **TR: B10**

◯ e-mail ◯ text messages ◯ nice color ◯ strong keys

◯ big screen ◯ wear and tear ◯ Wi-Fi ◯ games / apps

**2** **Listen.** Number the sentences. **TR: B11**

____ I told them that it cost me money.

____ I'll ask my son not to take it for a swim next time!

____ The clerk said that they tested everything.

1 Did you ask the clerk in the store if it was waterproof?

____ They told me to buy another one!

____ Did you ask them if they could fix it?

**3** **Work with a partner.** You want to return or exchange the broken phone. Act out a conversation.

Hello. Can I help you?

Yes, please. Yesterday I bought a cell phone in this store and . . . .

**4** **Work in groups of three.** Take turns. Ask and answer questions. Take notes.

1. Have you ever visited a waterfall or a lake? Where?
2. Which water creatures do you find interesting? Why?
3. How do you try to save water at home?
4. If you saw someone wasting water right now, what would you tell them?
5. Whenever you see a leaking faucet, what do you do?
6. Have you been swimming recently? Did you swim in salt water or in fresh water?

**5** **Work with another group.** Compare your information. How are you similar and different?

**6** **Read.** Match the questions and answers. Then put the words in parentheses in order.

QUESTIONS

1. Tiny bugs have been crawling on old books in our study. My son said they were booklice. Are there really booklice? What are they?
2. My daughter said that head lice only lived in dirty hair. Is this true?

ANSWERS

A: ____ No. They like all kinds, clean and dirty! However, these (gray / tiny / common) ______________________ insects prefer children between the age of four and eleven! They have long legs that help them crawl on human heads.

B: ____ He's right. These (brown / strange / light) ______________________ organisms usually live outdoors, but some other habitats include: libraries, closets, and other warm indoor places. Adults reach lengths of 1-2 millimeters.

**7** **Write.** Imagine you are a very small insect. Write a fun question about humans. Then write a short description of a human!

# Let's Talk

## I mean . . .

I will . . .

- ask a friend for help.
- give myself time to think.
- correct myself.
- show doubt.

**1 Listen and read.** TR: B12

Flavio: **Can you help me with** my homework, **guys? I'm confused.**

Paulo: **Sure,** Flavio. **What's the problem?**

Flavio: What's the difference between a tornado and a thunderstorm? **I don't get it.**

Paulo: **Well,** tornadoes bring heavy rain. **I mean,** they bring a lot of *wind,* not rain.

Joao: Yeah. And the wind moves very fast, in a circle.

Paulo: But a thunderstorm is different. There's lots of rain.

Flavio: **Are you sure? I always thought that** thunderstorms had lots of wind, too.

| | | | |
|---|---|---|---|
| **Can you help me with ________, guys?**<br>**I'm confused.**<br>**I don't get it.** | **Sure. What's the problem?**<br>Of course! Tell me. | **Well, . . .**<br>**I mean, . . .**<br>Let me think.<br>Hang on.<br>Um . . . | **Are you sure?**<br>Is that right?<br>I don't think so.<br><br>**I always thought that . . .**<br>I read that . . .<br>I heard that . . .<br>________ told me that . . . |

**2 Work in groups of three.** Use the chart. Discuss English words that you often find confusing. For example:

*history* and *story* *alone* and *lonely* *fun* and *funny*

# Actually, it's true.

I will . . .
- express surprise and disbelief.
- contest a fact.
- quote a source.
- agree to disagree / concede.

**3 Listen and read.** TR: B13

Dilek: Why don't we write about ants? There are more than 16,000 species of ants on the planet. And they're cool!

Leyla: No way! **Where did you get that idea?**

Dilek: **Actually, it's true.** And **according to the scientist Edward O. Wilson,** there might be even more species than that.

Leyla: **OK,** let's write about ants **then!**

| **Where did you get that idea?**<br>You can't be serious!<br>Sorry, but I don't see how that's possible. | **Actually, it's true.**<br>You know, there are many sources.<br>In fact, that's right. | **According to ______,**<br>Research shows that . . .<br>A study by ______ shows that . . . | **OK.**<br>**OK, ______ then!**<br>All right. Let's . . .<br>That's interesting.<br>I've never thought about that before. |
|---|---|---|---|

**4 Listen.** You will hear two discussions. Circle the answer. TR: B14

1. Who or what do the students quote?
   a. a website  b. a study  c. an explorer  d. their teacher
2. Who or what do the students quote?
   a. a website  b. a study  c. an explorer  d. their teacher

**5 Work with a partner.** Choose a situation and discuss.

1. I heard on TV that chocolate is good for you. Let's write about that.
2. Why don't we do a report on "BASE jumping"? You know, about 200 people have died doing this sport. I read it in a magazine.
3. Let's do a project on ancient Egypt. There are lots of articles on the National Geographic websites about it.

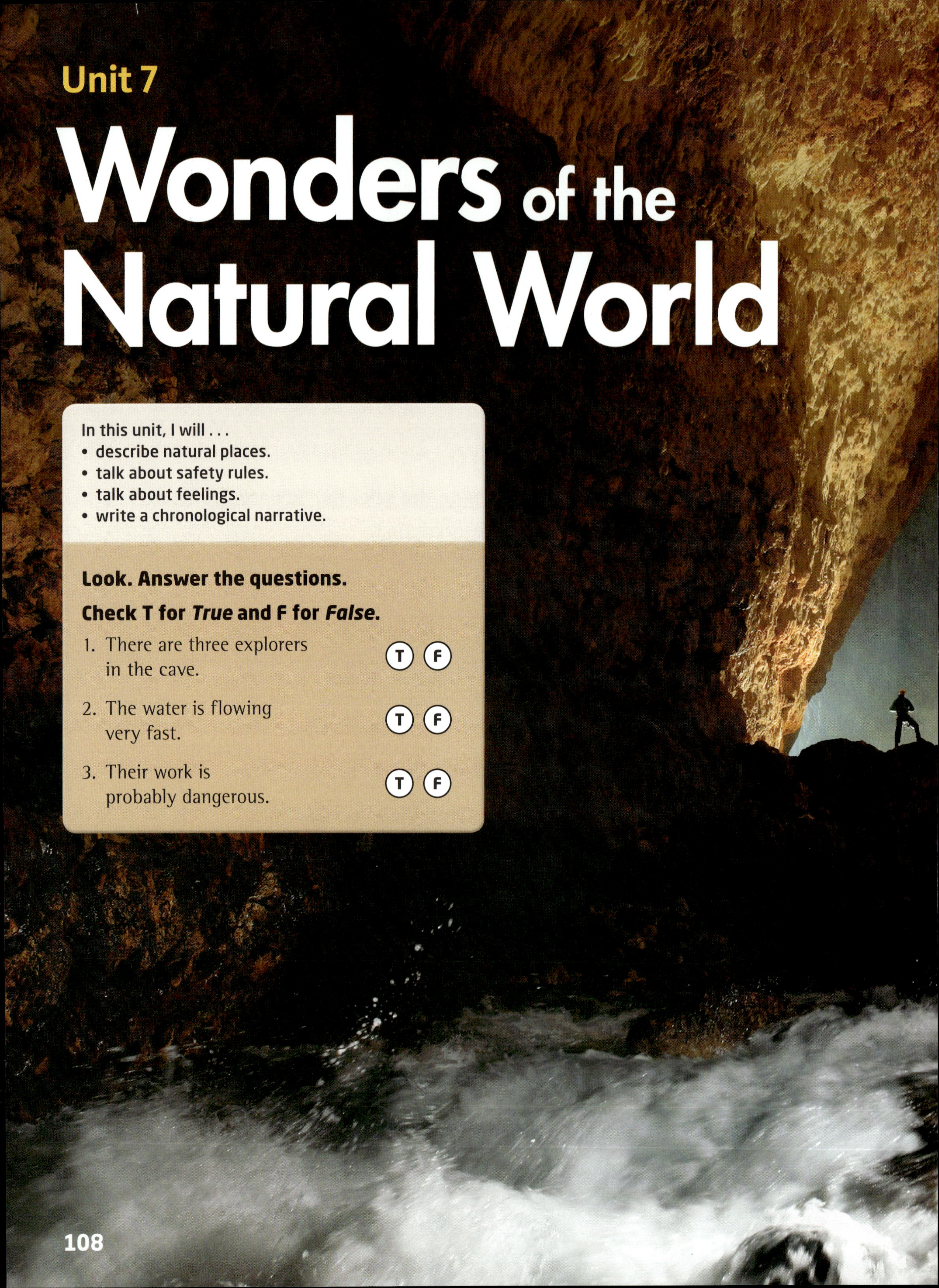

Unit 7

# Wonders of the Natural World

In this unit, I will . . .

- describe natural places.
- talk about safety rules.
- talk about feelings.
- write a chronological narrative.

**Look. Answer the questions.**

**Check T for *True* and F for *False*.**

1. There are three explorers in the cave. Ⓣ Ⓕ
2. The water is flowing very fast. Ⓣ Ⓕ
3. Their work is probably dangerous. Ⓣ Ⓕ

Ora Cave, New Britain Island,
Papua New Guinea

## 1 Listen and read. TR: B15

## 2 Listen and repeat. TR: B16

Explorers have dangerous jobs. They hike through jungles, **ascend** and **descend** steep mountains, or swim with sharks. They take big **risks** to learn more about our world.

Whenever Kenny Broad descends into a deep saltwater cave, he takes risks. Poisonous **underwater** gases fill the air. Broad needs **safety gear.** He wears a helmet for protection and uses a **headlamp** to **shine** on the cave. The **rope** helps him find his way.

Dan´s Cave, Abaco Island, Bahama Islands

Mireya Mayor is an outdoor scientist who observes wildlife. To find gorillas, she **crosses streams,** climbs mountains, and crawls along **tunnels.** Her work is sometimes very dangerous. Once she was even **chased** by a gorilla! Mayor believes anyone with **curiosity** can be an explorer.

Matthew Berger, son of famous explorer Lee Berger, made an amazing discovery in South Africa **by accident.** Nine-year-old Matthew was running after his dog when he **tripped over** and **located** the two-million-year-old fossil of a boy.

3 **Work with a partner.** What did you learn? Ask and answer.

## 4 Listen, read, and sing. TR: B17

# Let's Explore

*Let's go exploring!*

***Let's explore! Let's go inside a cave.***
***Let's explore! Be sure to be safe.***
***Let's explore! There's so much to see.***
***Don't forget your safety gear and curiosity!***

*We're inside a cave.*
*We're ready to climb down.*
*What should we use to keep us safe?*
*A rope can be used to help us descend.*
*A headlamp can be worn to help us light our way.*

*CHORUS*

*We're deep underwater,*
*and we want to ascend.*
*What should we use to help us stay safe?*
*A rope can be used to help us ascend.*
*Let's follow it to find our way back where we began.*

*When we're underwater in a jungle or a cave,*
*safety gear must be used to help us stay safe.*

*CHORUS*

*Let's explore!*

## 5 Answer the questions.

1. What two things should we take with us when we explore?
   a. safety gear b. ____________________
2. Check the safety gear that is not mentioned in the song.
   a. __ a headlamp b. __ a rope c. __ a helmet
3. Would you like to explore a cave? Why or why not? What place would you most like to explore?

   ________________________________________

Cave of Swallows, Mexico

## GRAMMAR TR: B18

Headlamps **must be worn** in dark caves.
Dangerous places **must not be entered** alone.

New species **have to be studied** in a science lab.
They **can't be analyzed** underwater.

**6** **Read and write.** Complete the paragraph.

The Nyiragongo volcano is beautiful but dangerous. If it erupts, it could kill the people who live below it. The people (1) __must be helped__ (must / help). Now! Because when a volcano starts to erupt, it (2) ________________ (can't / stop). To save lives, volcanic activity (3) ________________ (must / study). Rocks (4) ________________ (have to / collect) from inside the volcano. Before Sims and his team descend, they need safety gear. The safety gear (5) ________________ (have to / check). Rubber shoes (6) ________________ (shouldn't / use) because they melt in the heat! Special suits and gas masks (7) ________________ (must / wear) to protect the scientists against heat and poisonous gases. As Sims descends by rope, the sound of gases (8) ________________ (can / hear) below. It's scary. But he collects the rocks and ascends safely. Now he and other scientists can learn more about the volcano.

**7** **What do you think?** Write safety rules for tourists who visit these places. Use these words.

| | | | |
|---|---|---|---|
| volcano<br>jungle<br>mountain<br>underwater cave | suit<br>water<br>food<br>boots<br>helmet<br>rope | environment<br>risks<br>animals<br>headlamp<br>photos | wear<br>carry<br>protect<br>use<br>take |

1. ____________________
2. ____________________
3. ____________________
4. ____________________
5. ____________________
6. ____________________

**8** **Work in a group.** Compare your rules.

**9** **Listen and repeat.** Look at the pictures. Complete the paragraph. **TR: B19**

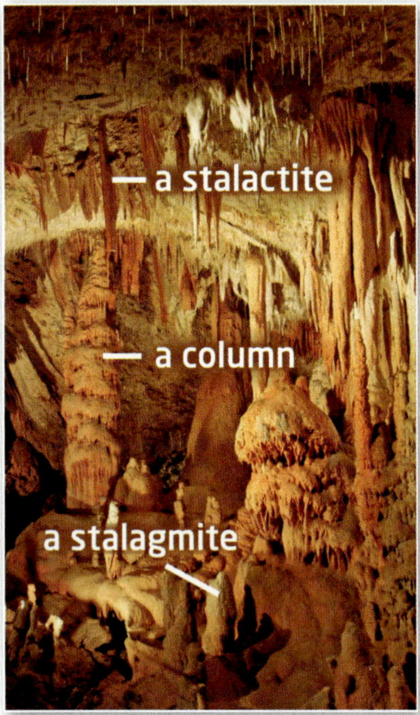

a bat

a painting

ancestors

Caves are full of life, such as bears, snakes, and (1) ________________. Caves used to be full of human life, too. We know that our (2) ________________ lived in caves thousands of years ago because they made (3) ________________ on the cave walls. In caves, water drips through the rocks to form stalactites and (4) ________________. They grow slowly. When a stalactite and stalagmite meet, they form a (5) ________________. This can take thousands of years! Here is an easy way to remember the difference. Stalagmites rise from the ground. (6) ________________ hang from the ceiling!

**10** **Listen and stick.** Work with a partner. **TR: B20**

| 1 | 2 | 3 | 4 | 5 |
|---|---|---|---|---|

## GRAMMAR TR: B21

Caves **make me** scared.
Heights **made her** nervous.

Exploring **makes Mireya** happy.
Matthew Berger **made his dad** proud.

**11** **Read.** Write sentences on a sheet of paper. Write about you, your family, and your friends.

| proud | scared | happy | sick | nervous | angry | tired | hungry |
|---|---|---|---|---|---|---|---|

1. *Thinking about chocolate makes me hungry!*
2. ______
3. ______
4. ______
5. ______
6. ______

**12** **Play a game.** Make the cubes on page 169. Play with a partner. Take turns. Make sentences.

**13** **Listen and read.** TR: B22

# Discoveries in the Dark

Explorer David Gill and his team are studying the beautiful island of New Britain, in Papua New Guinea. Some of the biggest river caves on Earth can be found here. During their two-month expedition, the team explores 13 kilometers (8 miles) of river caves, discovering waterfalls, lakes, and much more!

The team makes a base camp at the top of the "doline" (a large bowl carved by rainwater). They sleep here, surrounded by rainforest and the sounds of frogs and insects. To reach Ora Cave, the explorers must descend the doline. Before entering the caves, they check their safety gear. They need headlamps to explore the dark world of river caves. And they can't cross rivers without ropes.

Ora's upstream hike is difficult, and the river flows dangerously fast. Eventually it leads to a large cave, as big as a theater! The explorers shine their headlamps on the ceiling, which is more than 30 meters (100 feet) high. A beautiful blue lake lies below. Unfortunately, the explorers can't hike to Phantom Pot from Ora Cave because there is a rocky "sump" (an area where water drains back into the earth). So they have to descend another day to Phantom Pot Cave. This time, the explorers crawl for two hours through a tiny rocky tunnel. When they reach Lake Myo and the Myo Falls, they are tired and wet, but the view is truly incredible!

David Gill hopes that one day the Papua New Guinea government will create a conservation area to protect this wonderful place.

**weird but true**

**The Cave of Crystals in Mexico contains the world's largest natural crystals—one is as big as a school bus!**

## 14 Read and write.

1. How long do the explorers spend on New Britain Island? ____________________
2. What safety gear do they use? ____________________
3. Why can't they hike directly from Ora Cave to Phantom Pot Cave?

____________________

4. How can the government protect this island in the future?

____________________

## 15 **Read the text again.** Look at the cave diagram. Number the places below. Write 1-6.

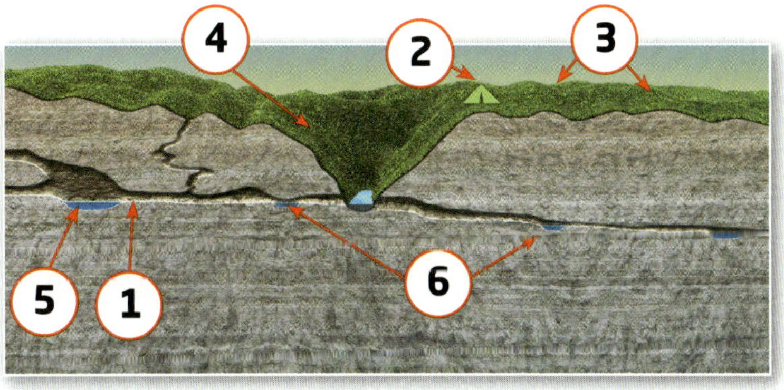


_____ base camp _____ doline _____ underground river

_____ Lake Myo _____ sump _____ rainforest

## 16 **Work with a partner.** Discuss some risks that the explorers could face on different parts of their journey. Compare your ideas with another pairs' ideas.

## Chronological Narratives

When you write a chronological narrative, you describe when each event happened. To make the story more interesting, you can set the scene and create suspense. To express the sequence of events, you can use time expressions such as *ago, afterward, immediately, suddenly,* or *then.*

**17** **Read.** Which time expression is not used in the narrative? How does the writer create suspense?

### Search for a Gorilla

A few years ago the explorer Mireya Mayor visited a jungle in Africa because she wanted to learn more about female gorillas. She joined some other scientists who were studying a male called "Kingo." Together they followed the gorillas everywhere. It was incredibly hot and the trail was difficult. First, there were bees in her face. Then she had to hike through mud for hours. At one point, when she was hiking through mud, she fell. She grabbed a tree, but she didn't know that there were ants in the tree. Hundreds of ants fell on her head, and they were crawling through her hair! They crawled under her clothes and bit her many times. It was horrible. But something amazing happened. Suddenly, she heard a female gorilla scream. She felt so excited. This was the female she wanted to find! She immediately forgot about bees, mud, and ants, and ran to find the gorilla. It was one of the most exciting moments of her life!

**18** **Write.** Imagine you are an explorer. Write about an adventure you had in a cave, a volcano, or the jungle. Remember to create suspense and describe the sequence of events.

**19** **Work in a small group.** Share your writing.

NATIONAL GEOGRAPHIC

# Mission

## Connect your school studies to the world.

- Work in a small group. Discuss what you have learned in science and geography recently.
- How are these topics useful in the real world? Write some ideas in the box.

- Work with another group. Share your ideas. Are they the same or different? Which ideas does everyone like best?

*"I am inspired by nature, and I try to take what I learn about nature and apply those lessons to design things people can use and to help us understand more about the world we live in."*

**Kakani Katija, Bioengineer**

Emerging Explorer

Mosaic jellyfish,
New South Wales, Australia

## 20 Make a diorama.

1. Work in a group of three.
2. Research some caves in the world. Choose one that interests you.
3. Learn how to make a cave diorama.
4. Find the materials you need.
5. Make the cave.

## Now I can . . .

- ◯ describe natural places.
- ◯ talk about safety rules.
- ◯ talk about feelings.
- ◯ write a chronological narrative.

## Unit 8

# Robots Rule

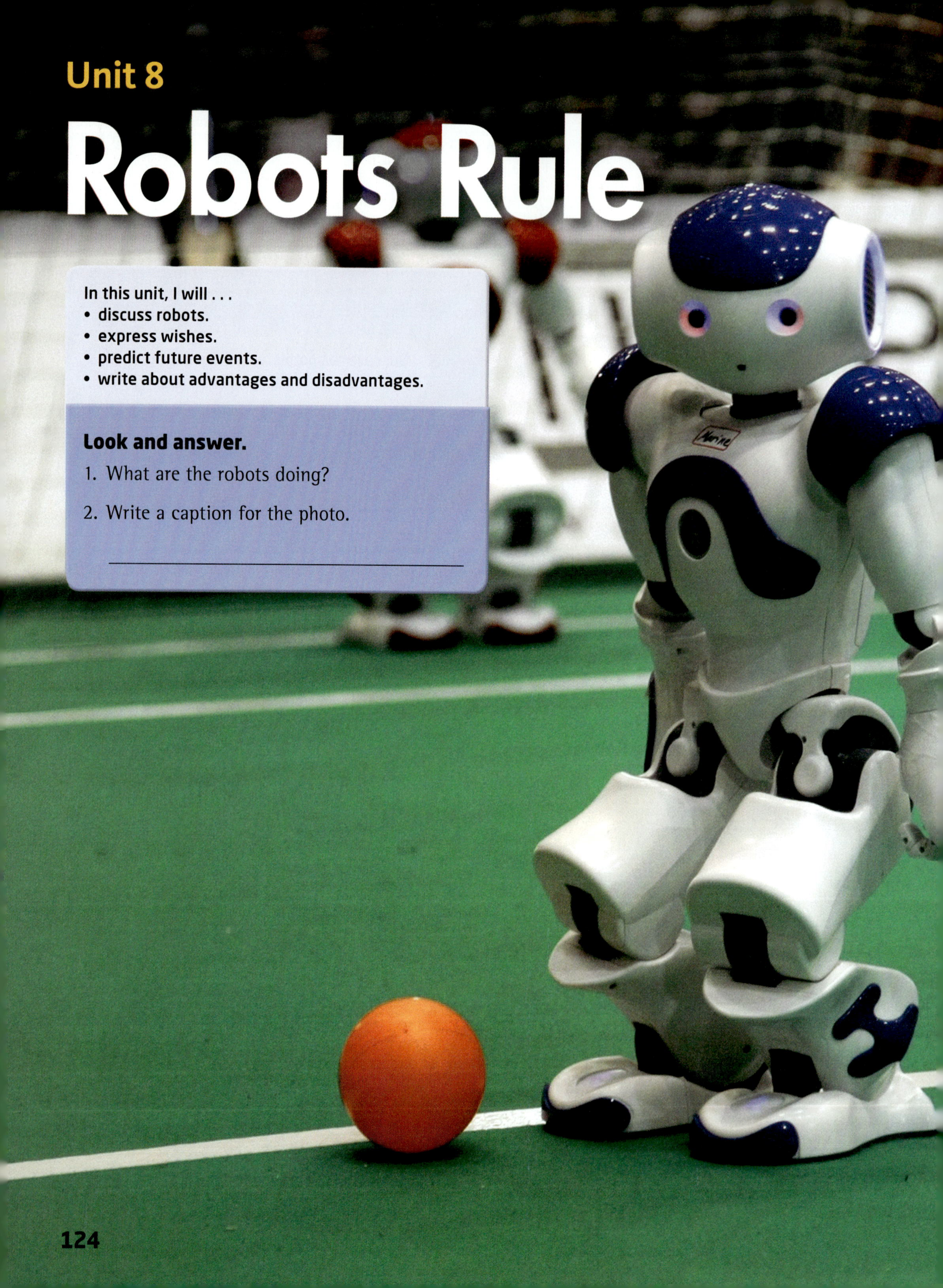

In this unit, I will . . .

- discuss robots.
- express wishes.
- predict future events.
- write about advantages and disadvantages.

**Look and answer.**

1. What are the robots doing?
2. Write a caption for the photo.

_______________________________

Robots playing soccer during RoboCup

## 1 Listen and read. TR: B23

## 2 Listen and repeat. TR: B24

Robots (or 'bots') are not just in **science fiction** movies. In real life, they work in many environments—in space, on land, and underwater. They do amazing jobs!

SPACE Robots can explore space easily because they are **mobile** and extremely **precise.** Also, they never need food or sleep. 'Bots' have successfully visited Mars, Venus, and Jupiter, where they were **controlled** by humans on Earth using **remote controls.**

Mars Rover

EARTH On Earth, robots are often used to perform useful **tasks** like cleaning and shopping. Robovie II is a Japanese shopping robot that helps people at the supermarket. Robots perform **social** tasks, too. For example, AIBO the dog is a wonderful **companion** for people. TOPIO, an android robot with human **features,** can even play table tennis.

UNDERWATER Bots do tasks that are too **dangerous** or **complex** for humans. They can **respond to commands** underwater, like collecting **information** about ocean life. Scientists hope to be able to **program** them to clean oil spills, too. Can robots help us save our oceans?

**3** **Work with a partner.** What did you learn? Ask and answer.

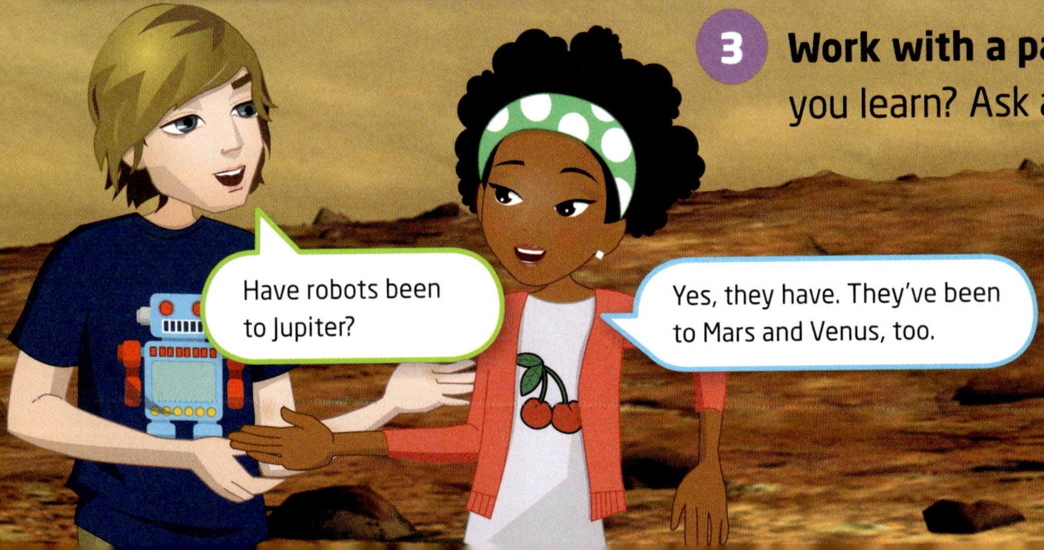

## 4 Listen, read, and sing. TR: B25

# I Am a Robot

*If I were a robot, what would my life be like?*
*I wish I were a robot! What would that life be like?*

*Now, I am a robot. I follow all commands.*
*But I wish I had more features.*
*I wish I had better hands.*

*Now, I am a robot. I do what I am told.*
*But I wish I had a birthday.*
*Then again, I never will get old.*

***I am a robot. I can do many things.***
***Have you ever met a robot that can sing?***

*Now, I am a robot. I'm helpful, and I'm smart.*
*But I wish that I could fix myself. I sometimes fall apart.*

*Now, I am a robot, made of wires and steel.*
*I always say the same thing if you ask me how I feel.*

***CHORUS***

*Now, I am a robot, and I must say goodbye.*
*But even when I'm sad, I am programmed not to cry.*

***CHORUS***

*Have you ever met a robot that can sing?*

## 5 Answer the questions.

1. Circle things that this robot would like to be able to do.
   a. follow commands
   b. have a birthday
   c. cry
2. Discuss. In what ways are robots similar to humans? In what ways are they different?
3. Discuss. Would you like to be a robot? Why or why not?

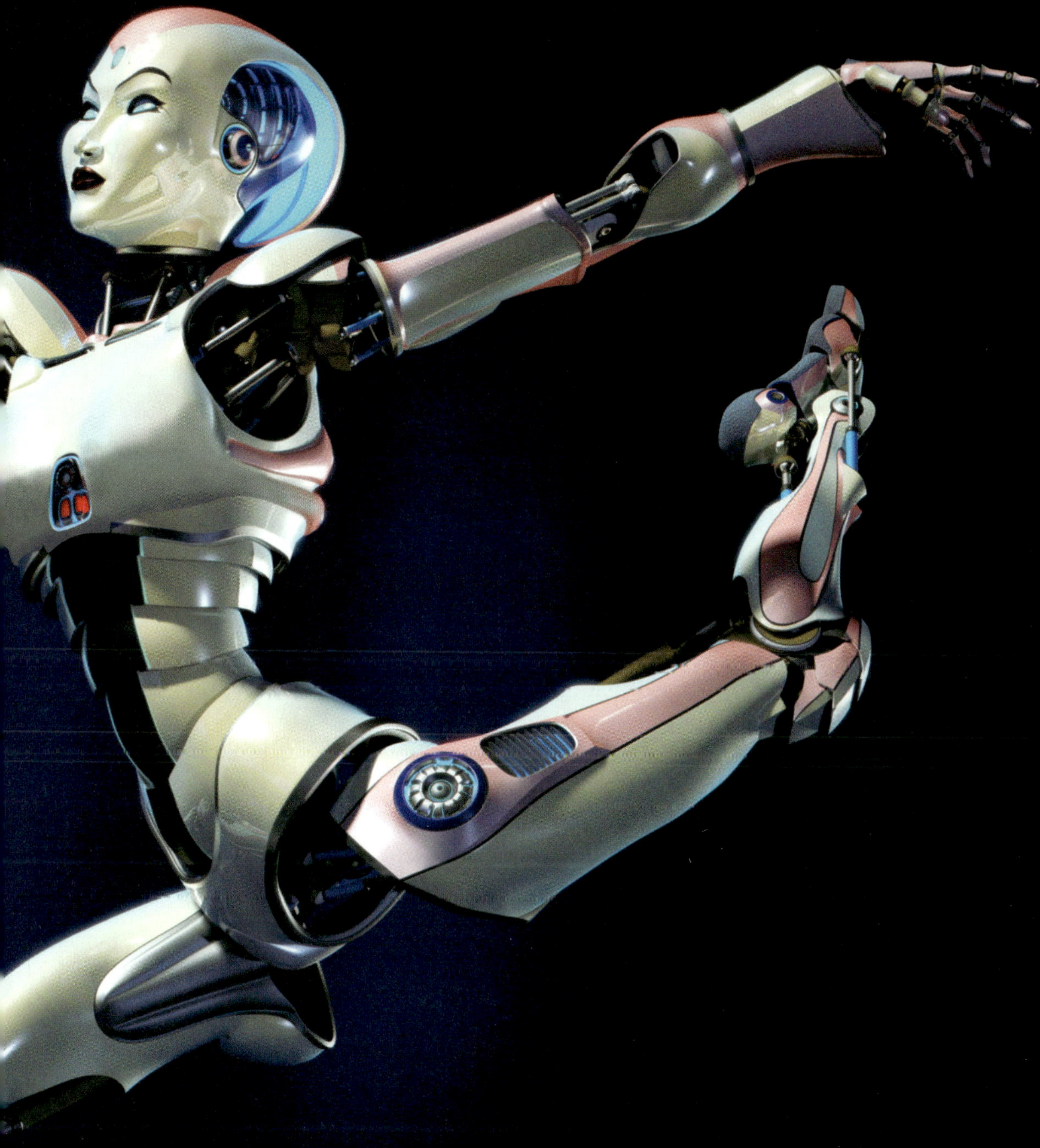

## GRAMMAR TR: B26

I wish my teacher **were** a robot. (But my teacher is not a robot!)
I wish I **could** program a robot. (But I can't.)
Dad wishes he **had** a robot that plays table tennis! (But he doesn't have one.)
Mom wishes the vacuuming robot **didn't cost** so much. (But it costs a lot.)

**6** **Read and write.** Complete the sentences.

1. I ____wish____ a personal robot ____could help____ (can / help) me speak English.
2. My family ________ there ________ (be) a robot to cook for us.
3. I ________ I ________ (not / have) to do everything myself. I'd like a personal robot!
4. My sister ________ she ________ (have) a robot to make snacks for her.
5. I ________ robots ________ (not / be) so expensive.
6. My cousins ________ they ________ (have) robots to make their beds!
7. I ________ I ________ (can) play table tennis like TOP10.
8. Our cat ________ my mom ________ (not / use) a vacuuming robot. He gets scared!

**7** **What about you?** What do you wish a robot could do for you? For other people? For plants and animals?

For me: I wish a robot could explain my homework to me.

For other people: I wish my grandmother had a robot shopper.

For plants and animals: I wish a robot could water the plants when we are on vacation.

**8** **Work with a partner.** Compare your wishes.

**9** **Listen and repeat.** Then listen and underline the missing words. **TR: B27**

# NEW! "Robo-Friend"

**The new "Robo-Friend" has many exciting features:**

She has **voice recognition.** She can understand you when you speak!

She has **facial recognition,** too. When she sees your face, she knows who you are.

Hundreds of **lasers** tell "Robo-Friend" what is in front of her, so she doesn't trip over.

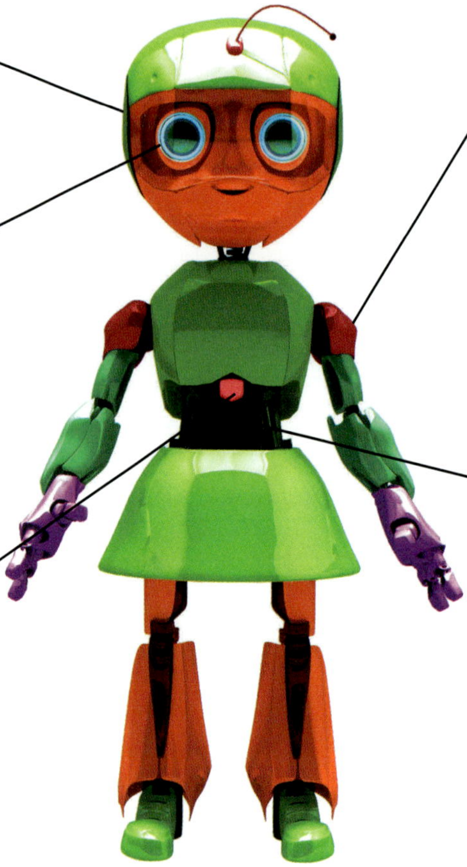

She has a **mechanical** arm. She can lift things for you.

She has thousands of **sensors.** She can feel, smell, and touch things.

1. sensors / voice recognition
2. mechanical / voice recognition
3. facial recognition / lasers
4. mechanical / lasers

**10** **Listen and stick.** Work with a partner. Discuss. **TR: B28**

Tell me about ASIMO. What can it do?

It has facial recognition. It can recognize the faces of 10 people.

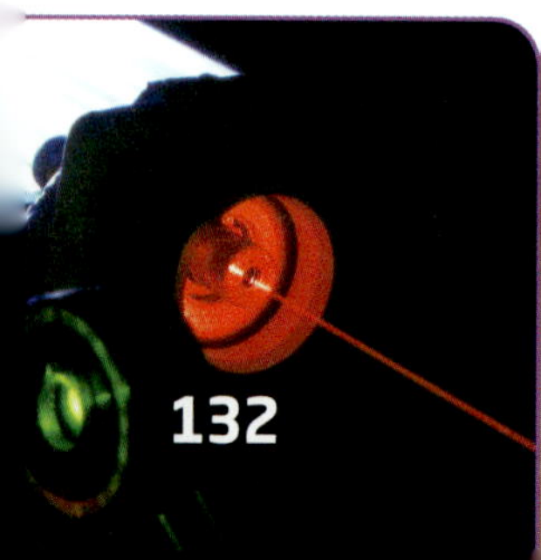
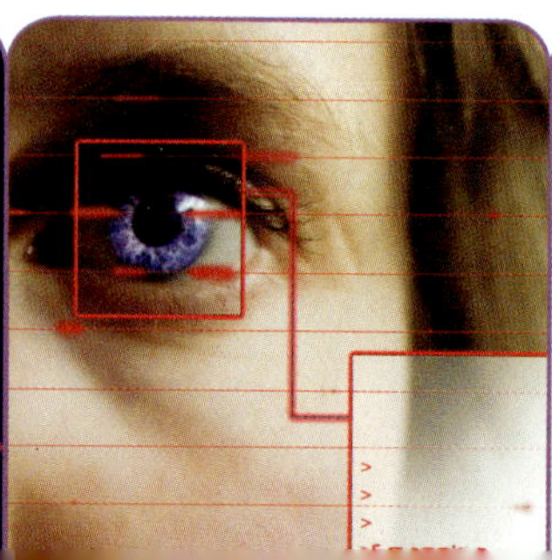

## GRAMMAR TR: B29

Robots **will be programmed** to do many of our dangerous jobs one day.
Most people **won't be required** to work more than a few hours a week.

**11** **Read and answer.** Complete the sentences about robots in the classroom. Check the ideas that you like.

1. Classroom robots ______________________ (give) complex sensors. They will hear us every time we talk in class.
2. Our class robot ______________________ (not / program) to understand voice commands in my language. When I need help, I will have to speak English.
3. Our robot ______________________ (teach) voice recognition. It will know my voice. When I need the robot's help, it will come to me.
4. Our class robot ______________________ (not / make) with just two mechanical arms. It'll have *lots* of arms.
5. The class robot ______________________ (train) in facial recognition. It will know when I am confused.

**12** **Play a game.** Use the game board on page 171. Play with a partner. Take turns. Predict what classroom robots and home robots will be like.

**Heads=** 1 space

**Tails=** 2 spaces

**13 Listen and read.** TR: B30

# Meet the Bots

Many people know that robots explore space and build things in factories. But did you know that there are many other kinds of robots? Let's meet some of these 'bots' and find out what they do.

Social robots are very popular. Wakamaru, a Japanese android robot, acts as a companion to elderly and disabled people. It can be programmed to remind people to take their medicine, and it can also call for help in an emergency. Robovie II helps people go shopping. Domestic robots (robots that clean your house) are very popular today, but they can be very expensive!

Medical robots are extremely important in modern medicine. With the da Vinci Surgical System, the doctor sits several feet away from the patient and controls the robot's every move. The HeartLander can do heart surgery. Thanks to robotics engineers, we also have prosthetic hands that work like human hands.

Service robots help in emergencies. The VGTV is a tiny vehicle that can rescue people who are trapped under fallen buildings. These robots use sensors to discover who is trapped, and then they send photos to the rescuers—all by remote control.

Explorer robots are incredibly useful, too. The Groundwater Voyager makes maps of underwater caves. And two Mars rovers, Opportunity and Curiosity, are exploring Mars. Amazing! What will future bots do?

weird but true

**A restaurant in China has robot waiters! They even smile when they visit the tables.**

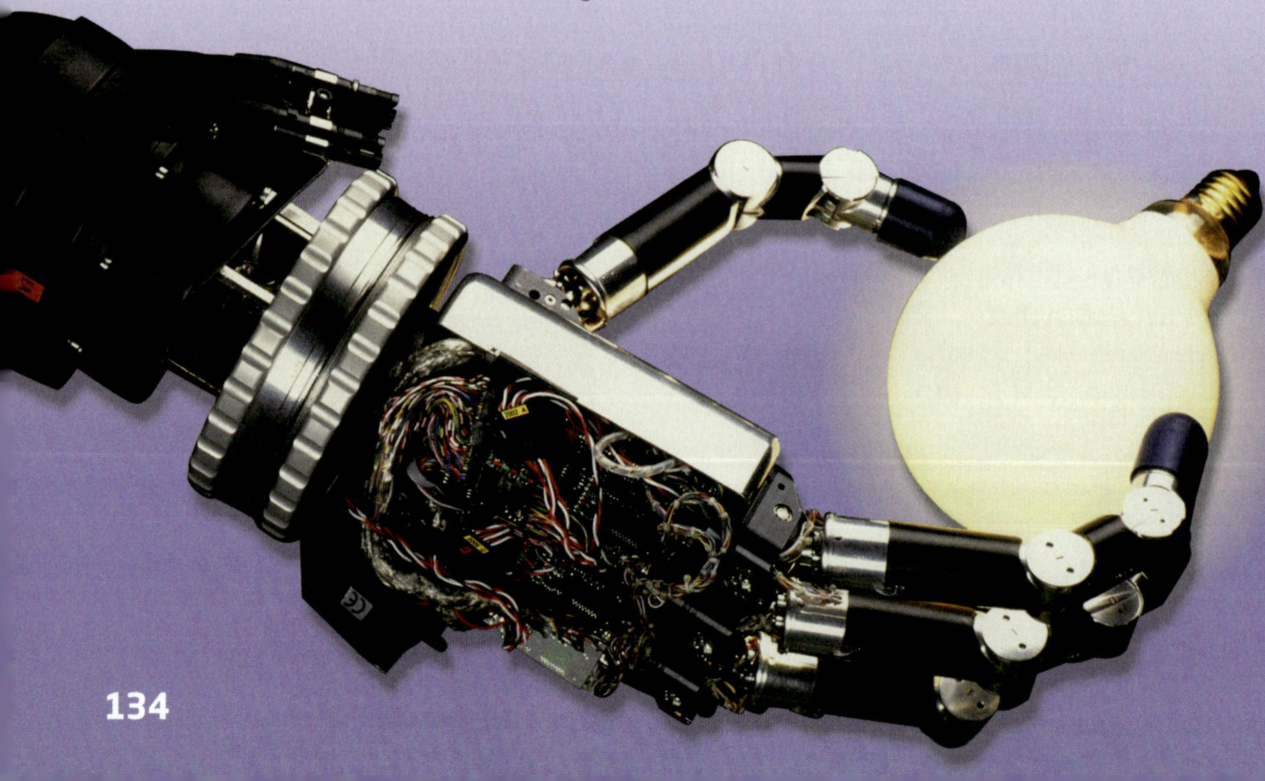

**14** **Answer the questions.** Check T for *True* and F for *False.*

1. Domestic robots are very expensive. (T) (F)
2. Prosthetic hands are identical to real hands. (T) (F)
3. Robotics engineers are people who design robots. (T) (F)
4. The HeartLander rescues people in buildings. (T) (F)

**15** **Complete the chart.** Write what each robot does. Check what kind of robot it is.

| | Function | Social | Medical | Service | Explorer |
|---|---|---|---|---|---|
| Wakamaru | It's a companion. | ✓ | | | |
| Robovie II | | | | | |
| da Vinci | | | | | |
| VGTV | | | | | |
| Groundwater Voyager | | | | | |

**16** **Work with a partner.** Discuss which type of 'bot' is the most . . .

useful. interesting.
complex. unnecessary.

## Paragraphs of Advantages and Disadvantages

When you write a paragraph of advantages and disadvantages, you should include at least two advantages and two disadvantages. To make your views clear, use expressions like *on the one hand, on the other hand, one (dis)advantage is . . .* , and *another (dis)advantage is . . .*

**17** **Read.** Read the paragraph. Underline the expressions that show advantages and disadvantages.

### Future Bots: Ready or Not?

Today bots are programmed and controlled by humans. But scientists are studying "artificial intelligence" (AI) robots. These robots will be able to think for themselves and do things without us. On the one hand, this is positive. For example, if an explorer robot finds something interesting in space, it can make a decision about it. Another advantage is that when a social robot breaks, it will know how to fix itself. On the other hand, there are risks. Are we ready for robots that can think by themselves? One disadvantage is that they might do things we don't want them to do. For example, they might send e-mails that are supposed to be from us! Another disadvantage is that AI bots won't know about behavior. They will need to be taught that some things are wrong, like stealing. If bots become too independent, the human world could become like a crazy science fiction movie!

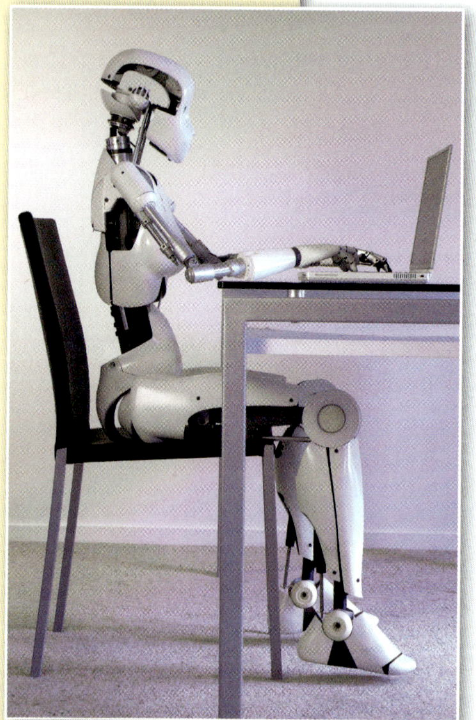

**18** **Write.** Write about the advantages and disadvantages of social robots as companions. Include two advantages and two disadvantages.

**19** **Work in a small group.** Share your writing.

NATIONAL GEOGRAPHIC

# Mission

## Use technology wisely.

- Work in a small group. What technology do you use every day?
- How does technology help us? What are some disadvantages of technology? Make two lists. Write your best ideas in the box.

- Work with another group. Share your lists. Are they the same or different? Which ideas does everyone like best?

*"From earliest times, humans had tools like hammers that extended our physical self. Today's technology extends our mental self. It's changing the way we experience the world."*

**Amber Case**

**Cyborg Anthropologist**

Emerging Explorer

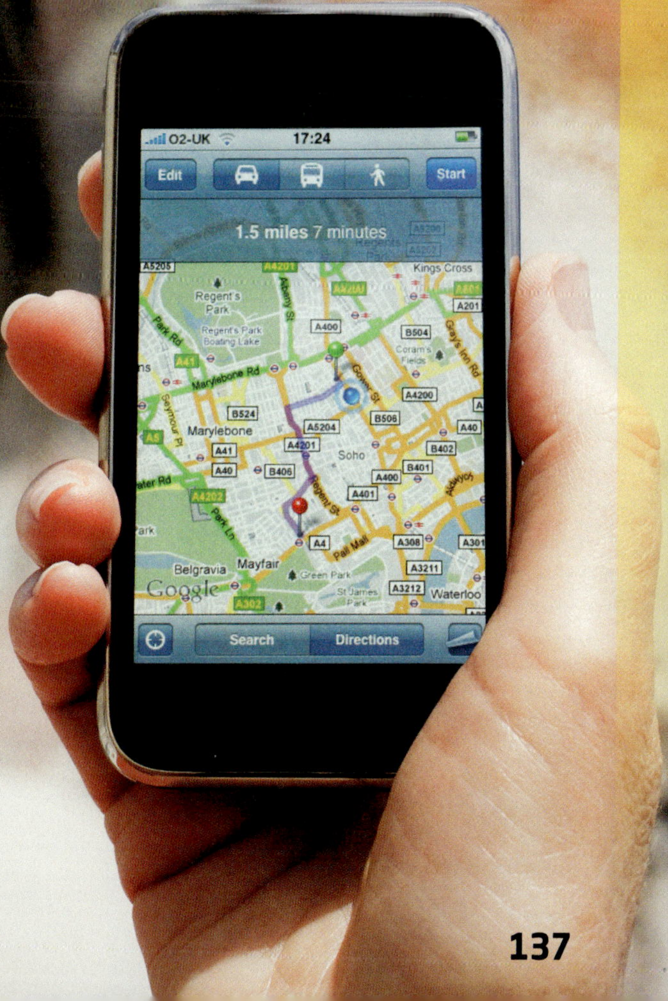

## 20 Design a robot.

1. Research personal robots.
2. Work in a small group. Imagine you could have a personal robot. Decide on some functions that you would like your personal robot to have.
3. Design a robot.
   a. Make a drawing of the robot.
   b. Label the features.
   c. Add information that explains what your new robot and its parts will look like.
   d. Discuss how your invention could have a positive impact.
4. Prepare a second drawing showing the robot doing its job.

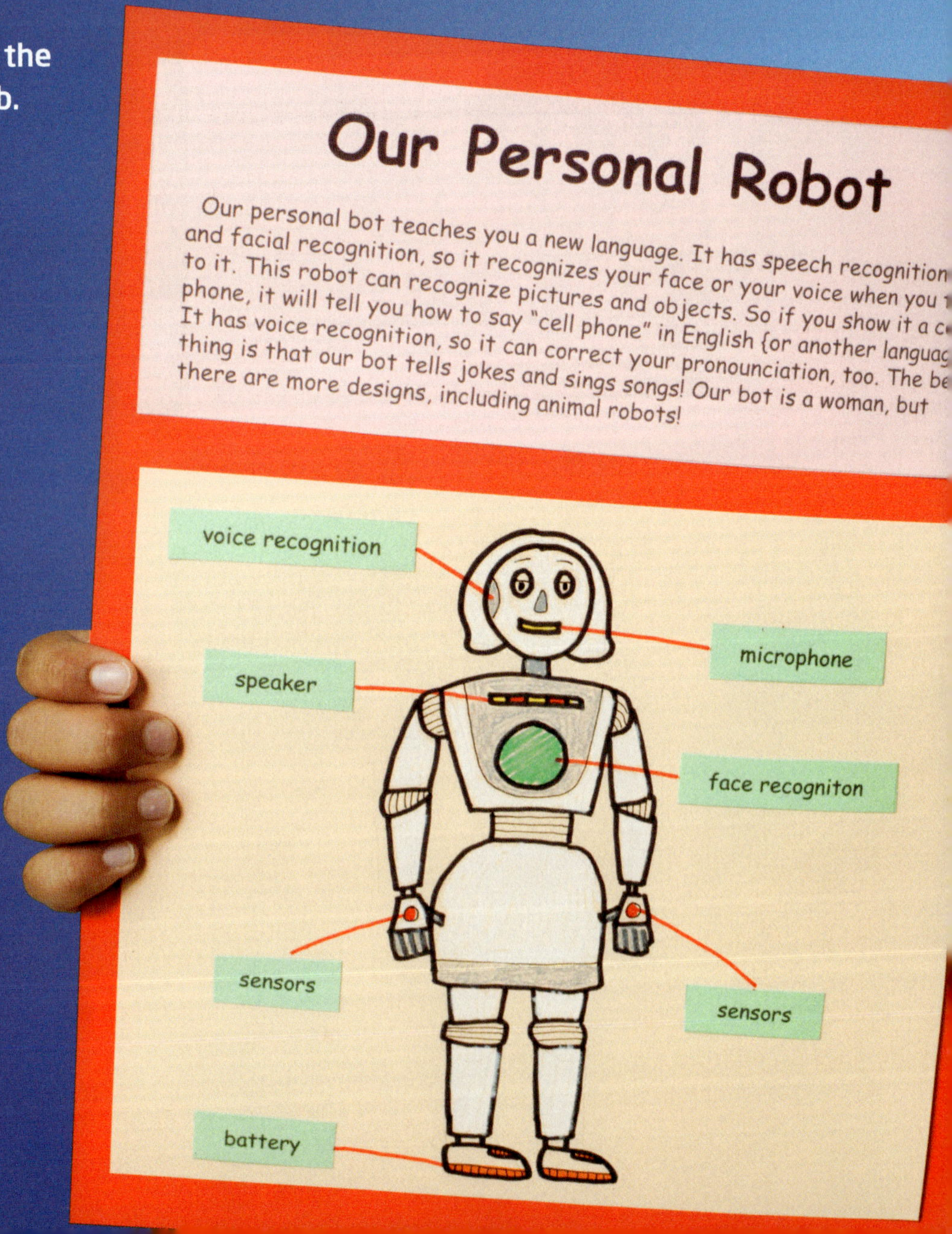

## Now I can . . .

- ◯ discuss robots.
- ◯ express wishes.
- ◯ predict future events.
- ◯ write about advantages and disadvantages.

Unit 9

# Amazing Adventures at Sea

In this unit, I will . . .
- discuss shipwrecks and their causes.
- tell stories about pirates.
- talk about deep-water exploration.
- write a paragraph of concession.

**Look and answer.**

1. What do you think of this shipwreck? Check all the words that apply.

   ◯ scary

   ◯ beautiful

   ◯ interesting

2. Would you like to explore a shipwreck?

   ◯ Yes, definitely.

   ◯ I'm not sure.

   ◯ No way!

*Titanic* shipwreck

## 1 Listen and read. TR: B31

## 2 Listen and repeat. TR: B32

More than a million **shipwrecks** lie on the ocean floor today. Many ships **sank** in bad weather, like the *Santa Margarita*, which was hit by a hurricane in 1622. What caused other shipwrecks?

Many centuries ago, ships carried **cargo** to sell to other countries. Ships also carried **weapons** because they were often attacked. In 1804, the Spanish ship *Nuestra Señora de las Mercedes* was attacked and exploded in a naval battle. It sank with over half a million **silver** coins.

**Pirates** were a big problem. In 1717, a famous pirate called Blackbeard **captured** the French ship *La Concorde*. By 1718, Blackbeard was **captain** of four stolen ships and had captured over 300 **sailors!** According to **legend,** he buried many treasures, but they have never been found.

The most famous modern shipwreck is the *Titanic*, which hit an **iceberg** and sank in 1912. There weren't enough **lifeboats** on board and over 1,500 people **drowned,** including most of the male **passengers** and **crew.** James Cameron, the director of the movie *Titanic*, has **dived** more than thirty times down to the shipwreck's site.

**3** **Work with a partner.** What did you learn? Ask and answer.

## 4 Listen, read, and sing. TR: B33

# Blackbeard

***Blackbeard, Blackbeard,***
***where's your silver now?***
***You've buried many treasures***
***that never have been found.***
***Blackbeard, Blackbeard,***
***I am going down***
***to the bottom of the sea***
***where treasure might be found.***

*I'm not afraid of icebergs. I'm not afraid to drown.*
*I'm the bravest sailor for miles and miles around!*
*As soon as I am captain, with cargo and crew,*
*I'll find your treasure deep in the ocean blue!*

***CHORUS***

*Local legend says there's a shipwreck near.*
*As soon as I am ready, I'm going there.*
*I love sunken treasure like flowers love rain.*
*I'm going to dive down again and again.*

*Heave-ho! Here we go!*
*Get the silver! Get the gold!*
*Heave-ho! Here we go!*
*Get the treasure down below!*

***CHORUS***

*Blackbeard, Blackbeard, where's your silver now?*

## 5 Check T for *True* and F for *False*.

1. No one has found Blackbeard's treasure. (T) (F)
2. The singer has been looking for it. (T) (F)
3. Write a new title for the song.

______________________________________

## GRAMMAR TR: B34

**As soon as** the *Santa Margarita* sank, people began looking for the silver.
Water poured into the *Titanic* **as soon as** it hit the iceberg.

**6** **Read and write.** Read the sentences. Write *"1"* above the action that happened first. Write *"2"* above the action that happened next. Rewrite and join the sentences.

1. A member of the crew saw the iceberg. He informed the captain.

As soon as a member of the crew saw the iceberg, he informed the captain.

2. The sailors heard about the iceberg. They tried to sail in a different direction.

________________________________________

3. The side of the *Titanic* was damaged. The ship hit the iceberg.

________________________________________

4. The water entered. The ship began to sink.

________________________________________

5. The ship began to sink. Many people fell into the freezing cold water.

________________________________________

**7** **What about you?** Work in pairs. Ask the questions. Write answers in the chart.

| What did you do as soon as you . . . | Me | My partner |
|---|---|---|
| 1. finished breakfast today? | | |
| 2. finished lunch yesterday? | | |
| 3. left school yesterday? | | |
| 4. finished dinner last night? | | |
| 5. went to bed last night? | | |
| 6. woke up this morning? | | |
| 7. had breakfast yesterday? | | |
| 8. left home this morning? | | |

**8** **Work in a new group.** Read and discuss. Compare your activities. Were they the same or different?

## 9 **Listen and repeat.** Underline the correct word. TR: B35

**correct**

**incorrect**

**safe**

**unsafe**

**legal**

**illegal**

**possible**

**impossible**

1. Captains shouldn't put a lot of cargo on ships. The ships might sink. It is (safe / unsafe).
2. These days it is (legal / illegal) to sail without a list of passengers. Captains must have a list of everyone who is on the ship.
3. It is (possible / impossible) to know what happened to some ships. We have found lots of information at the shipwrecks.
4. According to legend, Blackbeard used to decorate his ships with human bones. That's (correct / incorrect). Of course he didn't do that!

## 10 **Listen and stick.** Tell your partner what each sign means. TR: B36

When you are on a ship, life jackets keep you safe.

That's right. Stick *safe* under picture 1.

## GRAMMAR TR: B37

**It is** important / useful / necessary / helpful **to** know how to swim.
**It is not** legal / safe / right **to** take artifacts from this shipwreck.
**It is** illegal / unsafe **to** be a pirate.

## 11 Read and write.

| | | |
|---|---|---|
| wrong / throw | impossible / know | important / wear |
| ~~Interesting / dive~~ | illegal / sail | unsafe / swim |

1. It is interesting to dive near shipwrecks. They are amazing habitats for sea creatures.
2. ____________________ a life jacket when you go sailing.
3. ____________________ how many people died on the *Doña Maria*. There was no passenger list.
4. ____________________ without a license. But some people still do it.
5. ____________________ trash in the ocean.
6. ____________________ with sharks.

## 12 **Play a game.** Cut out the cards on page 173, and use the game board on page 175. Place the cards face down in a pile. Work in a small group. Take turns. Follow the route, pick a card, and make a sentence.

**13** **Listen and read.** TR: B38

# Journey to the Bottom of the Earth

James Cameron, the famous explorer and movie director, traveled to the deepest point of the Mariana Trench—the Challenger Deep—on March 26, 2012. At about 11,000 meters (about 36,000 feet) below sea level, this is the deepest point on Earth. Since childhood, Cameron has wanted to dive and explore the ocean. Now he has reached the deepest point in the ocean. Alone.

**Weird but true**

**In the *DEEPSEA CHALLENGER*, all the water vapor from Cameron's breath was condensed and stored in a plastic bag so that Cameron could drink it in an emergency!**

The Mariana Trench is perhaps the most isolated place on the planet. Because of its extreme depth, the pressure at the bottom of the Mariana Trench is incredibly strong. The temperature is just a few degrees above freezing, and the place is always in darkness. Although two explorers went there in 1960, Cameron was the first to film this strange, dark place.

For this incredible expedition, Cameron traveled in a submersible called the *DEEPSEA CHALLENGER*. It was 7.3 meters (24 feet) long and 1.09 meters (43 inches) wide—so small that Cameron could hardly move. Yet the sub was powerful enough to reach the bottom of the ocean in just two hours and thirty-six minutes and ascend in seventy minutes! In the *DEEPSEA CHALLENGER*, Cameron spent three hours filming the bottom of the ocean while its mechanical arms picked up rocks and animals.

We know less about the deepest points on our planet than we do about the surface of Mars. But the samples Cameron collected will give scientists a lot of information. When they analyze the rocks, they might discover more about the shape of the land and the earthquakes that cause tsunamis. And by studying the organisms that survive there, perhaps scientists can even learn more about how life began!

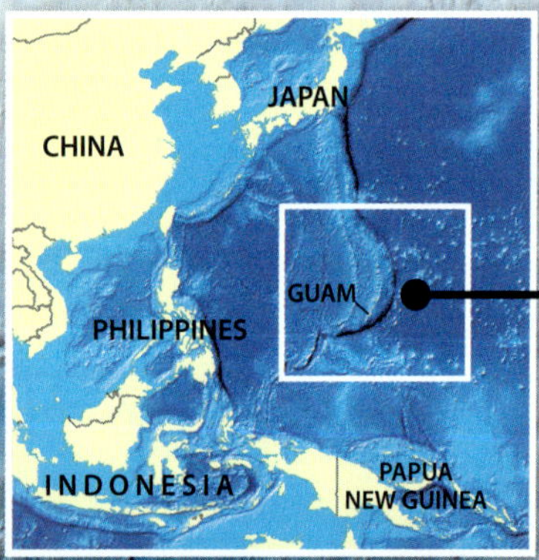

## 14 **Read.** Circle the answer.

1. Cameron was the ________________ person to dive to the Mariana Trench.

   (a) first (b) second (c) third

2. He had dreamed about this journey since he was ________________.

   (a) born (b) a boy (c) 15 years old

3. There was ________________ room inside the *DEEPSEA CHALLENGER.*

   (a) no (b) not much (c) lots of

4. The rocks from the Mariana Trench could teach us about ________________.

   (a) earthquakes (b) organisms (c) the next dive

## 15 **Reread the text.** Complete the Fact File.

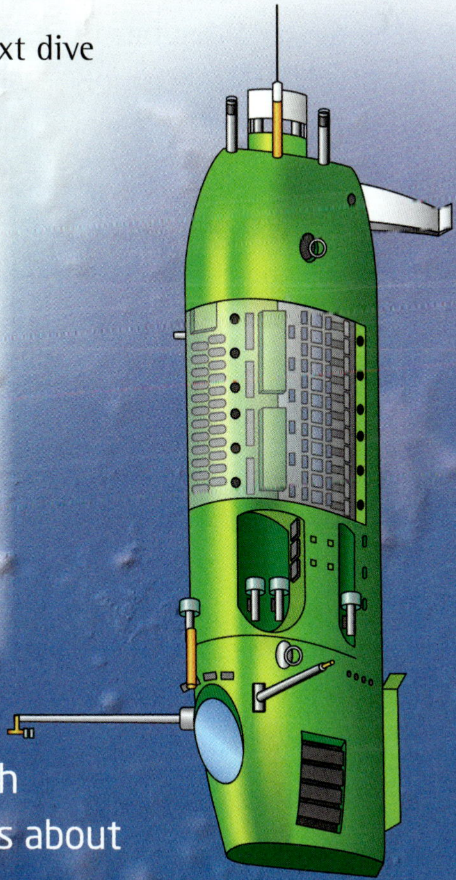

### THE DEEPSEA CHALLENGER

Length ________________

Width ________________

Depth traveled ________________

Descent time ________________

Ascent time ________________

## 16 **Work in pairs.** Role play an interview with James Cameron. Ask and answer questions about these topics.

James Cameron

Journey to the Mariana Trench

Mariana Trench

*DEEPSEA CHALLENGER*

Importance of the expedition

## Paragraphs of Concession

In a paragraph of concession, you discuss opinions. You also accept that different points of view may be partially correct. When you use concession, you can use words such as: *even though*, *granted that*, or *while it may be true*.

**17** **Read.** Underline the words of concession used in this paragraph.

### Whose Treasure Is It?

In 2007, an American shipwreck salvage company discovered over 500,000 silver coins in a shipwreck in the Atlantic Ocean. The silver is from the Nuestra Señora de las Mercedes, a Spanish ship that sank when it was attacked in 1804. Who does the treasure belong to today? The Spanish government says that the silver is theirs, but is it? While it may be true that the ship was Spanish, it was carrying the silver from Peru. And the Peruvian government says the silver is theirs because the coins were made with Peruvian silver. So, whose is it? Granted that the explorers who discovered the treasure are from the USA, there is an agreement between the USA and Spain stating that all silver from Spanish shipwrecks must go back to Spain. So even though three countries wanted this treasure, it now belongs to Spain.

**18** **Write.** Write about the objects found in the *Titanic* shipwreck. Do the objects belong to the explorers, the relatives of survivors, or museums? Use expressions of concession.

**19** **Work in a small group.** Share your writing.

NATIONAL GEOGRAPHIC

# Mission

## Be a lifelong learner.

- What do you dream of doing?
- How can you prepare for it? Think of ideas. Take notes in the box.

*"There are thousands of undiscovered shipwrecks and ancient sites in Cuba. It's an immense field of work waiting for archaeologists to explore."*

**Daniel Torres Etayo**
**Archaeologist**
Emerging Explorer

- Work with a partner. Share your ideas. Are they the same or different?

## 20 Plan your first exploration.

1. Work with a partner. Choose something or someplace that you would like to explore together.
2. Plan your first exploration.
   a. What do you need to know about the topic before you go on your expedition? Make a list. Discuss how you can research more information.
   b. Choose some people (for example, scientists) who should go with you on your trip.
   c. List what you need to take with you on your trip.
3. Make a poster.

We're planning a trip to the Caribbean to find an old shipwreck. It was one of Blackbeard's ships!

## Now I can . . .

- ◯ discuss shipwrecks and their causes.
- ◯ tell stories about pirates.
- ◯ talk about deep-water exploration.
- ◯ write a paragraph of concession.

# Review

## 1 **Listen to the story.** Check the ship. TR: B39

| | The *Doña Paz* | The *Vector* | Neither |
|---|---|---|---|
| 1. Attacked by pirates | | | ✓ |
| 2. Crossed the ocean in 1987 | | | |
| 3. Carried oil | | | |
| 4. Carried weapons and silver | | | |
| 5. Had too many passengers on board | | | |
| 6. Sank | | | |
| 7. Sailors died in the fire | | | |
| 8. The captain didn't have a license. | | | |

## 2 **Listen again. Match.** TR: B40

1. Shipwrecks make Amy feel ____
2. The *Doña Paz* captain was wrong. He allowed too many passengers on board. It was ____
3. The fire started as soon ____
4. It's impossible to know ____
5. Ben wishes that he ____
6. Amy wishes that he ____

a. how many people died.
b. sad.
c. would be quiet sometimes.
d. could dive underwater and explore the shipwreck.
e. as the two ships crashed.
f. illegal and unsafe.

## 3 **Work with a partner.** Imagine you were on board the *Vector* or the *Doña Paz*. Describe what happened. Take turns. Ask and answer questions.

**4** **Read.** Match the sentence halves.

1. A headlamp ______
2. Stalactites and stalagmites ______
3. This stream ______
4. One day this robot ______
5. Tunnels ______

a. will be programmed to think for himself.
b. can't be crossed.
c. must be worn in the cave.
d. must not be touched.
e. can be found underground.

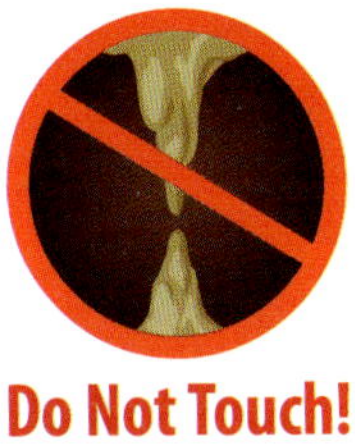

**5** **Write.** Choose four objects from the list. Write clues for your partner.

| | |
|---|---|
| bat | pirate |
| caves | safety gear |
| iceberg | remote control |
| information | science fiction movies |
| painting | underwater robots |

*This can be used to turn off the TV.*

*These robots descend to the bottom of the sea.*

**6** **Work in a group.** Take turns. Read your clues to your partners. Can they guess? Win a point for each correct guess!

| | | | |
|---|---|---|---|
| must (not) be | has to be | ascend | find |
| can be | will be | control | touch |
| can't be | won't be | descend | use |

# Let's Talk

## See what I mean?

I will . . .
- open a conversation.
- state an opinion and clarify it.
- check understanding.
- confirm an opinion.

**1 Listen and read.** TR: B41

Ahmed: **You know,** I don't think we need to practice handwriting anymore. In the future, we won't need to write.

Yusef: **Really? Why do you say that?**

Ahmed: **Well,** in the future we'll just talk to the computer and it will write for us! **I mean,** no one is going to write by hand in a few years. So, it doesn't make sense to practice handwriting now. **See what I mean?**

Yusef: **What? Are you saying that** we won't need to write any notes either? No writing at all?

Ahmed: Well, of course people will write by hand sometimes! **What I mean is . . .**

| | | | | |
|---|---|---|---|---|
| **You know,**<br>You know what? | **Really? Why do you say that?**<br>You think so?<br>Why's that? | **Well,** ___<br>**I mean,** ___<br>You see, ___ | **See what I mean?**<br>Do you see what I mean?<br><br>**What I mean is** ___<br>What I meant was ___ | **What? Are you saying that** ___ **?**<br>So you're saying that ___ ?<br>So are you saying that ___ ? |

**2 Work with a partner.** Use the chart. Discuss a future change that you believe will happen.

# Please take a look.

I will . . .
- refer to visuals in a presentation.
- invite questions from the audience.
- end a presentation.

## 3 Listen and read. TR: B42

Natalie: So, **please take a look at** our poster. **This shows** something you can make for your home.

Fernand: **You'll notice that** it is made from just a simple object.

Natalie: This is a good example of recycling.

Fernand: Now, **would anyone like to ask any questions?**

Natalie: OK, **that concludes our presentation.**

Fernand: And **our time's up. Thanks for listening,** everyone.

| **Please take a look at** ____<br>Now, let's look at ____<br>Here's a picture of ____<br>This chart shows ____ | **You'll notice that** ____<br>If you look closely, you'll see that ____<br>As you can see, ____ | **Would anyone like to ask any questions?**<br>Are there any questions?<br>Does anyone have any questions? | **Thanks for listening.**<br>**That concludes our presentation.**<br>**Our time's up.** |
|---|---|---|---|

## 4 Listen. You will hear two discussions. What are the two students showing the class? Circle the answer. TR: B43

1. a. a poster b. a book c. some photos d. an invention or model
2. a. a poster b. a book c. some photos d. an invention or model

## 5 Work in pairs. Prepare and practice presentations.

1. You are showing the class something you made using recycled materials.
2. You are showing the class a poster with photos from an archaeological site.
3. You are showing the class an invention.

# Irregular Verbs

| Infinitive | Simple Past | Past Participle |
|---|---|---|
| be | was/were | been |
| beat | beat | beaten |
| become | became | become |
| begin | began | begun |
| bend | bent | bent |
| bite | bit | bitten |
| bleed | bled | bled |
| blow | blew | blown |
| break | broke | broken |
| bring | brought | brought |
| build | built | built |
| buy | bought | bought |
| catch | caught | caught |
| choose | chose | chosen |
| come | came | come |
| cost | cost | cost |
| cut | cut | cut |
| dig | dug | dug |
| do | did | done |
| draw | drew | drawn |
| drink | drank | drunk |
| drive | drove | driven |
| eat | ate | eaten |
| fall | fell | fallen |
| feed | fed | fed |
| feel | felt | felt |
| fight | fought | fought |
| find | found | found |
| fly | flew | flown |
| forget | forgot | forgotten |
| forgive | forgave | forgiven |
| freeze | froze | frozen |
| get | got | gotten |
| give | gave | given |
| go | went | gone |
| grow | grew | grown |
| hang | hung | hung |
| have | had | had |
| hear | heard | heard |
| hide | hid | hidden |
| hit | hit | hit |
| hold | held | held |
| hurt | hurt | hurt |
| keep | kept | kept |
| know | knew | known |
| leave | left | left |
| lend | lent | lent |
| let | let | let |
| lie | lay | lain |
| light | lit | lit |
| lose | lost | lost |
| make | made | made |
| meet | met | met |
| pay | paid | paid |
| put | put | put |
| read | read | read |
| ride | rode | ridden |
| ring | rang | rung |
| rise | rose | risen |
| run | ran | ran |
| say | said | said |
| see | saw | seen |
| sell | sold | sold |
| send | sent | sent |
| set | set | set |
| sew | sewed | sewn |
| shake | shook | shaken |
| shine | shone | shone |
| show | showed | shown |
| shut | shut | shut |
| sing | sang | sung |
| sink | sank | sunk |
| sit | sat | sat |
| sleep | slept | slept |
| slide | slid | slid |
| speak | spoke | spoken |
| spend | spent | spent |
| spin | spun | spun |
| stand | stood | stood |
| steal | stole | stolen |
| stick | stuck | stuck |
| sting | stung | stung |
| stink | stank | stunk |
| sweep | swept | swept |
| swim | swam | swum |
| swing | swung | swung |
| take | took | taken |
| teach | taught | taught |
| tear | tore | torn |
| tell | told | told |
| think | thought | thought |
| throw | threw | thrown |
| understand | understood | understood |
| wake up | woke up | woken up |
| wear | wore | worn |
| win | won | won |
| write | wrote | wrote |

| Infinitive | Simple Past | Past Participle |
|---|---|---|
| light | lit | lit |
| lose | lost | lost |
| make | made | made |
| meet | met | met |
| pay | paid | paid |
| put | put | put |
| read | read | read |
| ride | rode | ridden |
| ring | rang | rung |
| rise | rose | risen |
| run | ran | ran |
| say | said | said |
| see | saw | seen |
| sell | sold | sold |
| send | sent | sent |
| set | set | set |
| sew | sewed | sewn |
| shake | shook | shaken |
| shine | shone | shone |
| show | showed | shown |
| shut | shut | shut |
| sing | sang | sung |
| sink | sank | sunk |
| sit | sat | sat |
| sleep | slept | slept |
| slide | slid | slid |
| speak | spoke | spoken |
| spend | spent | spent |
| spin | spun | spun |
| stand | stood | stood |
| steal | stole | stolen |
| stick | stuck | stuck |
| sting | stung | stung |
| stink | stank | stunk |
| sweep | swept | swept |
| swim | swam | swum |
| swing | swung | swung |
| take | took | taken |
| teach | taught | taught |
| tear | tore | torn |
| tell | told | told |
| think | thought | thought |
| throw | threw | thrown |
| understand | understood | understood |
| wake up | woke up | woken up |
| wear | wore | worn |
| win | won | won |
| write | wrote | wrote |

| | | | |
|---|---|---|---|
| Go forward one space! | How many types of chocolate bars are there today? | When is International Chocolate Day? | Where do cacao trees grow? |
| What do farmers open to take out cacao seeds? | Go back two spaces! | Name one type of chocolate filling. | Why was a recipe printed? (so that...) |
| What's your favorite type of chocolate? | When was the first chocolate candy bar made? | Go back two spaces! | Name three ingredients in chocolate. |
| Go forward one space! | Why did Joseph Fry add new ingredients to chocolate? (so that...) | Why was sugar added to chocolate? (so that...) | Go back two spaces! |

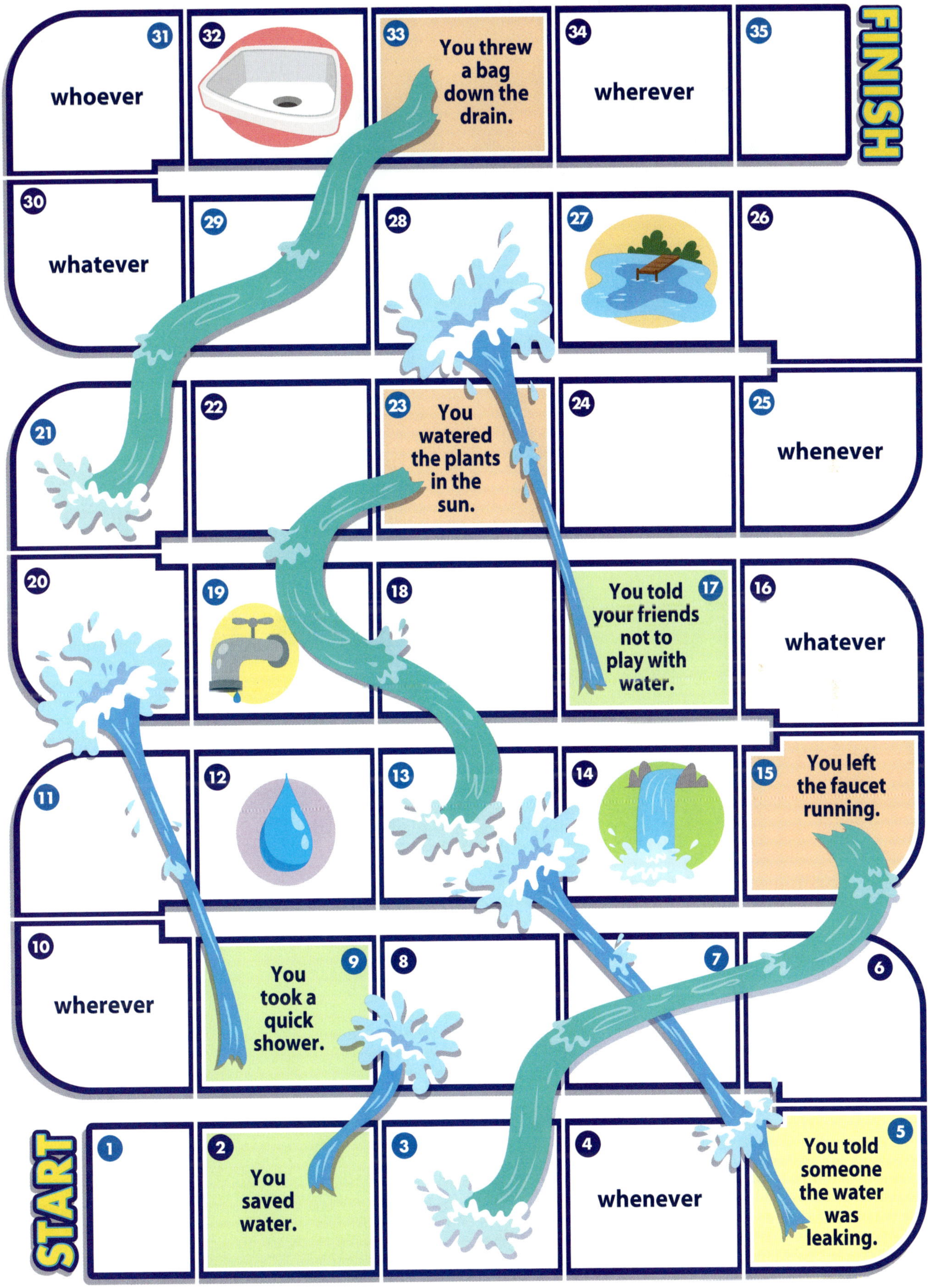
START
1
2
You saved water.
3
4
whenever
5
You told someone the water was leaking.
6
7
8
9
You took a quick shower.
10
wherever
11
12
13
14
15
You left the faucet running.
16
whatever
17
You told your friends not to play with water.
18
19
20
21
22
23
You watered the plants in the sun.
24
25
whenever
26
27
28
29
30
whatever
31
whoever
32
33
You threw a bag down the drain.
34
wherever
35
FINISH

Where is the computer store?

Can you show me your backpack?

Where can I buy this phone?

Can I have a bicycle for my birthday?

Where can I buy a toy car like this?

Can you help me?

What do we need to buy next?

Do you like these jeans?

How much do these sneakers cost?

Do you have a tablet?

Can I help you?

Do you have a TV with a large screen?

glue

nervous

glue

angry

happy

scared

proud

glue

glue

excited

glue

glue

glue

my best friend

glue

my parents

me

you

my teacher

glue

glue

us

glue

glue

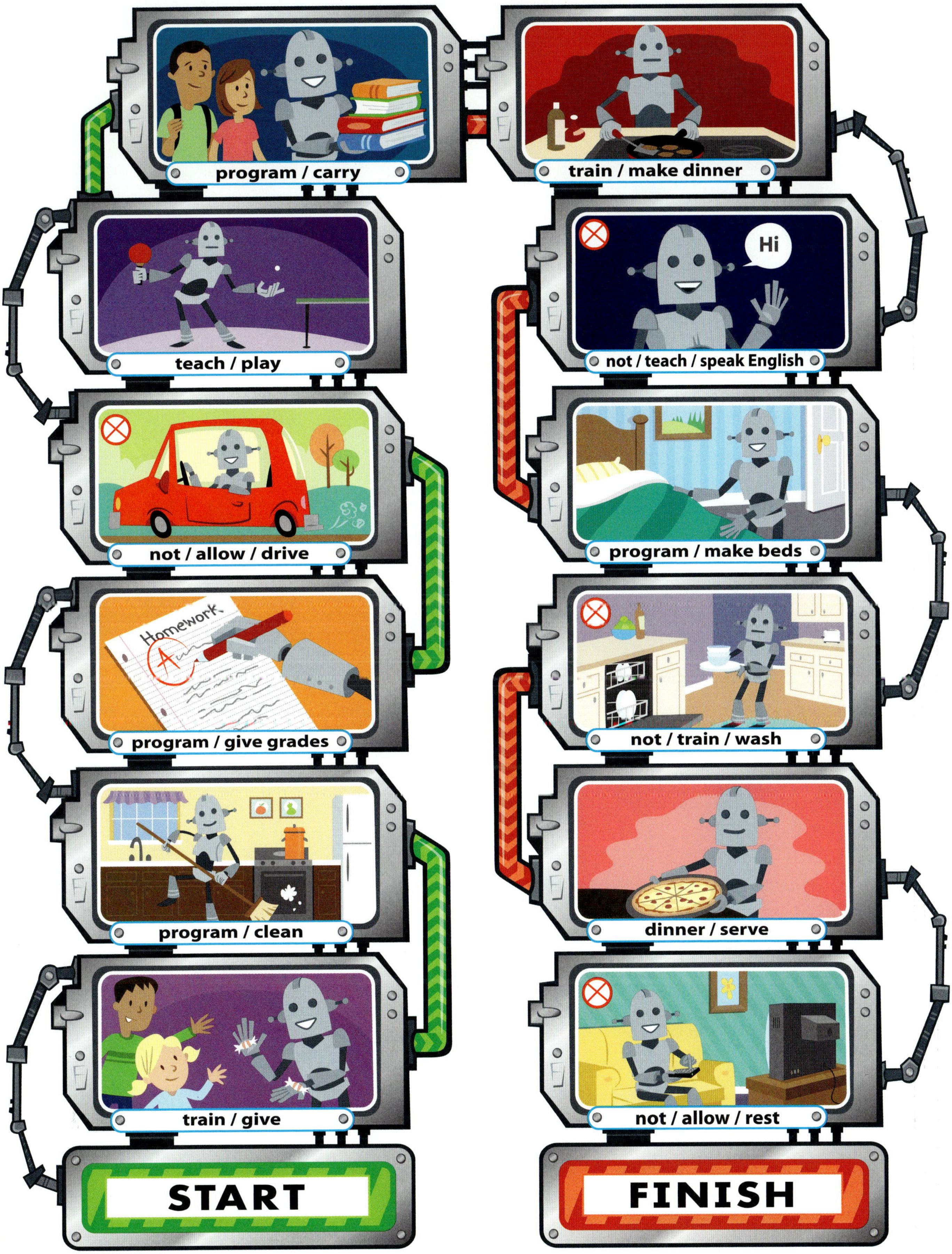
program / carry
train / make dinner
teach / play
Hi
not / teach / speak English
not / allow / drive
program / make beds
Homework
program / give grades
not / train / wash
program / clean
dinner / serve
train / give
not / allow / rest
START
FINISH

**You are captured by pirates. Go back three spaces.**

**Sharks are attacking your ship. Miss a turn.**

important / wear life jacket

interesting / learn about

important / wear bike helmet

interesting / discover

**You find some treasure! Move forward three spaces.**

**There is a big storm. Go back two spaces.**

important / listen to

interesting / read about

important / study English

possible / drown

**The wind is blowing in the right direction. Move forward two spaces.**

**Your ship has a leak. Miss a turn.**

unsafe / swim alone

possible / discover creatures

unsafe / go out late

impossible / know

**You capture a famous pirate. Move forward two spaces.**

**Many of your sailors are sick. Go back two spaces.**

unsafe / run

impossible / go

unsafe / try to save a friend in the water

illegal / take artifacts

| | | | |
|---|---|---|---|
| useful / have | useful / wear | necessary / have | illegal / cross |
| necessary / study | exciting / explore | exciting / watch | fun / make |
| right / save | not right / waste | not right / pollute | fun / watch |
| right / recycle | useful / know | | |

FINISH
24
23
22
21
20
19
18
17
Pick a wild card
15
14
13
Pick a wild card
7
6
9
Pick a wild card
11
10
5
Pick a wild card
START
1
2
3
N
W
E
S

**Unit 1**
stickers

**Unit 2**
stickers

same family | ate meat | were sick | were rich | lived close by

DNA test | samples | CT scan | artifacts | the site

**Unit 3**
stickers

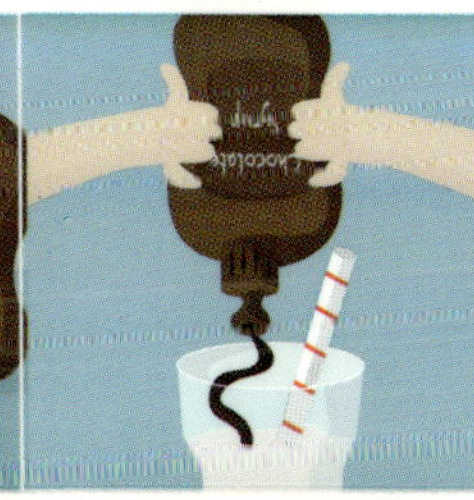

**Unit 4**
stickers

**Unit 5**
stickers

## Unit 6
stickers

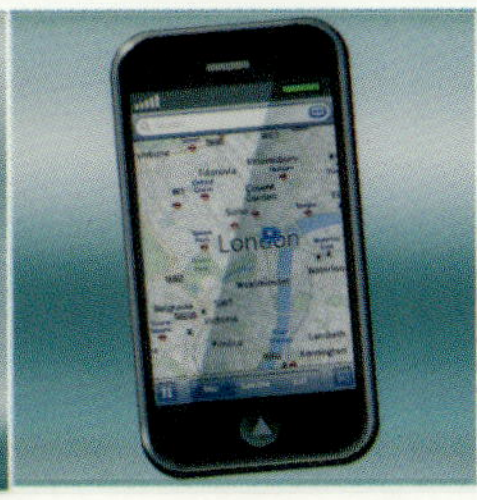

## Unit 7
stickers

## Unit 8
stickers

mechanical

lasers

voice recognition

sensors

facial recognition

remote control

command

companion

## Unit 9
stickers

unsafe

possible

impossible

illegal

safe

legal

incorrect